FRANCE

THE BEAUTIFUL
COOKBOOK

One hundred best recipes by
THE SCOTTO SISTERS

Text by
GILLES PUDLOWSKI

CollinsPublishersSanFrancisco
A Division of HarperCollinsPublishers

Published in the U.S.A. in 1994 by
Collins Publishers San Francisco
1160 Battery Street San Francisco, CA 94111 USA

Conceived and produced by Weldon Owen Inc.
814 Montgomery Street San Francisco, CA 94133 USA

President: John Owen
Publisher: Jane Fraser
Project Editor: Ruth Jacobson
Editor: Janet Mowery
Editorial Assistant: Kim Green
Index: Ken DellaPenta
Design and Art Direction: John Bull
Design Layout: Ruth Jacobson
Color Illustration: Nicole Kaufman
Black and White Illustrations: Yolande Bull
Production: James Obata, Stephanie Sherman
Food Photography: Peter Johnson, Pierre Hussenot
Food Styling: Janice Baker, Laurence Mouton

ISBN 0-00-255464-X

The Beautiful Cookbook® series is a
registered trademark of Weldon Owen Inc.

Production by Mandarin Offset, Hong Kong
Printed in Hong Kong

Above: In port cities like La Rochelle, diners looking forward to a *plateau de fruits de mer,* a platter of raw and cooked shellfish,
can be assured of its freshness. Pages 4–5: Baked Zucchini with Tomatoes and Cheese (top left, recipe page 95),
Stuffed Zucchini Flowers (top right, recipe page 95) and Vegetable Fritters (center front, recipe page 93), photographed in Provence.
Pages 8–9: The Loir, a tributary of the famous Loire River, flows through the tiny village of Les Roches L'Évêque.

Photographs by Pierre Hussenot/Agence Top: pages 4–5, 6, 10, 15, 18–19, 23, 29,
32, 35, 36, 42, 46–47, 51, 52, 61, 62, 65, 66, 79, 83, 84, 98, 108–109
Photographs by Peter Johnson: pages 12, 17, 20, 24, 26, 27, 30, 38, 41, 45, 48, 54, 57, 59,
69, 71, 73, 74, 76, 80, 87, 88, 90, 92, 97, 100, 103, 104, 106, 110, 112, 115, 116, 118
Photographs by Leo Meier: pages 2, 8–9

CONTENTS

INTRODUCTION

In France, every road leads to a splendid food. From Flanders (Flandres) to the Basque country (Pays Basque), from Normandy (Normandie) to Nice, from Ardennes to southernmost Bigorre, the worthy hexagon is unequaled in its flavors. This book bears witness to France's infinite richness, a richness that embraces ancient regional traditions (zealously retained in spite of new administrative boundaries), the landscape, the flavors of its foods, and the methods of preparation particular to each small area.

Beer and charcuterie predominate in eastern France, fresh vegetables and garden herbs in the south. It is easy to discern two faces in France: the domain of butter and the domain of oil, which correspond, more or less, to north and south. Butter cuisine is heavier; fresh oil is lighter, more digestible. *Andouillettes* and poultry sizzle in butter; oil—from the olive in the southeast, the walnut in the southwest—caresses the fish of the Mediterranean.

Through history, the French predilection for fine cooking has never faltered. Spices were highly esteemed in the Middle Ages but rejected at the start of the Renaissance, when the flavors of exotic seasonings were replaced by those of indigenous herbs: onions, shallots, garlic, *rocambole*. Mushrooms were honored, truffles worshiped.

Thus the French discovered the resources of their own country, but mostly kept them for themselves. The classic texts written around the end of the seventeenth century—such as *Le Cuisinier Français*—advocated the selection of natural ingredients and the use of crunchy vegetables—asparagus for example—with an *al dente* style of cooking. The nineteenth century was the boomtime of the great Parisian restaurants (Café de Foy, Véry, Café Français) and of rich and ornate cuisine, always highly sauced.

"Rediscover yesterday's flavors with today's techniques": this could be the motto of the cuisine of the present era. Now, at the end of the twentieth century, all the traditions of France have been thoughtfully brought together: the diverse regional cuisines, the bourgeois cuisine restoring to honor the old, slow-simmered dishes *(blanquette, daube, navarin, pot-au-feu)*, preserving with jealous care the great classics of the country. The *bouillabaisse* of Marseilles, the *aïoli* of Provence, the *bourride* of southern France, the *cassoulet* of the southwest—as well as the preserved goose and *foie gras* of Périgord, the *choucroute* of Alsace, the *potée* of Lorraine, the tripe of Normandy, and the *aligot* of Auvergne—are but a few of the unique culinary masterpieces that the year 2000 should preserve and promote as supreme examples of French genius.

SWISS CHARD PIE (TOP, RECIPE PAGE 117), PASTRY PUFFS (RIGHT, RECIPE PAGE 102) AND LEMON TART (BOTTOM, RECIPE PAGE 114)

FIRST COURSES

A TYPICAL MEAL IN FRANCE today consists of a first course, a main dish, cheese (which is eliminated by those in a hurry or considered as the final course by those on a diet), and dessert. On special occasions, three dishes are served before the cheese—generally a cold hors d'oeuvre, a hot first course and then the main dish.

Hot first courses often take the form of *tourtes, quiches, pâtés, hures* and *soufflés*. These are rich, contrived dishes that typically demand a complicated, or at least elaborate, preparation. It is a mark of respect to one's guests to offer them such a dish, to which much care and attention will have been devoted in the kitchen well before their arrival.

First courses often depend heavily on meat and fish. Eggs, too, are treated in a multitude of styles, according to region: with peppers in the Basque country, as *pipérade;* as truffle omelettes in Provence and Tricastin; poached in red wine as *oeufs en meurette* in Burgundy or *couilles d'âne* in Berry. These dishes are perfect examples of the diversity of preparations that the richness of the French countryside allows for a single ingredient.

Often vegetables are the centerpiece. Mediterranean artichokes, which might be stewed in oil, *à la barigoule,* contrast with Breton artichokes, which are simply eaten with a vinaigrette sauce. Asparagus, whether from the Vaucluse, the Loire Valley or Alsace, here slender and green, there large and white, is always served with *mousseline* sauce, mayonnaise or vinaigrette. Yet in the east it will be accompanied by ham, and in the Midi it will accompany a main dish. In general, the first courses offered north of the Loire—the line that divides France both climatically and gastronomically—are more substantial, more robust, richer than in the south.

A few first courses have become quite separate dishes, like the *foie gras* that is served cold as an hors d'oeuvre, but that might be pan-fried and served warm, accompanied by fruits that have been tossed in butter. And certain dishes that might otherwise have been served as the main course have been accepted as light first courses, such as raw meats prepared in the manner of the Italian *carpaccio.*

Some regions have a reputation for abundant first courses, as prelude to a rich and copious meal. Others have retained a tradition of light, fresh-tasting first courses. Often these are the maritime regions, where salads—such as the *salade niçoise* of Nice—or seafood constitute the most natural of preludes to a meal.

Regardless, in any self-respecting French meal, the first course has a single role: to inspire in the diner the desire to pursue his pleasant task.

PUMPKIN SOUP (RECIPE PAGE 21)

OLIVE SPREAD

Provence

TAPENADE
OLIVE SPREAD

The name of this dish derives from the word tapeno, *which is the Provençal equivalent of* câpres *(capers). In fact Toulon capers are an indispensable ingredient of this wonderfully flavored sauce.*

6 anchovies preserved in salt
13 oz (400 g) black olives in brine, pitted
1 small clove fresh, young garlic, coarsely
    chopped
3 tablespoons capers, rinsed and drained
2 teaspoons strong mustard
2 tablespoons cognac
freshly ground pepper
⅔ cup (5 fl oz/150 ml) extra virgin olive oil
country bread or rye bread

❧ Rinse the anchovies under cold running water and rub them to remove all traces of salt. Separate into fillets, removing the head and backbone. Cut each fillet into small pieces.
❧ Combine the anchovies, olives, garlic and capers in a food processor. Add the mustard, cognac, pepper and half the oil and blend to a thick paste; while continuing to blend, pour in the rest of the oil. When the *tapenade* is smooth, transfer it to a serving bowl.
❧ Serve as an appetizer with slices of country bread or rye bread, plain or toasted. *Tapenade* may be kept for several days in the refrigerator.

Serves 6

Provence

ANCHOÏADE
ANCHOVY SPREAD

12 anchovies preserved in salt
6 cloves fresh, young garlic, finely chopped
3 fresh, young French shallots, finely chopped
1 tablespoon red wine vinegar
¾ cup (6 fl oz/200 ml) extra virgin olive oil
6 sprigs parsley, stemmed and finely chopped
raw vegetables: celery, cauliflower, radishes,
    fennel, artichokes, peppers (capsicums) . . .
slices of baguette (French bread), toasted

❧ Rinse the anchovies under cold running water and rub them to remove all traces of salt. Separate into fillets, removing the head and backbone. Cut each fillet into small pieces.
❧ Combine the chopped anchovies, garlic and shallots in a food processor. Add the vinegar and blend until smooth. With machine

running, pour in the oil in a thin stream, then add the parsley and blend for 10 seconds longer. Serve the *anchoïade* spread as a dip for raw vegetables and on toasted slices of bread.

Serves 6   *Photograph pages 18–19*

Provence

SOUPE AU PISTOU
VEGETABLE SOUP WITH BASIL-GARLIC PASTE

In the Provençal dialect, pistou *means not basil, but* pilé—*the Italian* pesto *of Genoese origin—a paste that includes ground basil and garlic, bound with olive oil. This soup is made all along the Mediterranean coast in summer, when the fresh haricot beans arrive at the markets. Each family has its favored recipe, and different vegetables are often used.*

2 lb (1 kg) fresh haricot beans or 1 lb (500 g) dried haricot beans, soaked overnight and drained
8 oz (250 g) fresh broad beans or 4 oz (125 g) dried broad beans, soaked overnight and drained
4 oz (125 g) green beans
8 oz (250 g) small zucchini (courgettes)
2 cloves fresh, young garlic
8 oz (250 g) boiling potatoes
8 oz (250 g) ripe tomatoes
2 onions, chopped
1 sprig basil
salt
3 oz (100 g) soup pasta or small macaroni
3 oz (100 g) Emmenthaler or Parmesan cheese, freshly and finely grated

FOR THE *PISTOU:*

8 oz (250 g) ripe tomatoes
1 large bunch basil, stems removed
4 cloves fresh, young garlic, quartered
6 tablespoons (3 fl oz/90 ml) fruity olive oil

❧ Shell the haricot and broad beans, if fresh, and remove the soft green skin that covers them. String the green beans (if necessary); wash and pat dry. Trim and quarter the zucchini lengthwise, then cut into ¼-in (5-mm) slices. Crush the garlic with a blow of the hand or with the side of a cleaver. Peel and wash potatoes; cut into ½-in (1-cm) cubes. Drop the tomatoes into boiling water for 10 seconds, then cool under running water. Peel, halve and squeeze out the seeds; coarsely chop the flesh.
❧ Combine all the vegetables with the garlic, onions and basil in a 4-qt (4-l) saucepan and cover with cold water. Bring to boil over gentle heat. Season with salt, cover and let simmer very slowly for 1 hour.
❧ When the soup is cooked, remove the garlic and basil. Add the pasta and cook until *al dente.*
❧ Meanwhile, prepare the *pistou:* drop the tomatoes into boiling water for 10 seconds, then cool under running water. Peel, halve and squeeze out the seeds; coarsely chop the flesh and let drain in a colander.
❧ Combine the basil, garlic, oil and tomatoes in a food processor or blender and blend to a smooth purée. When the pasta is cooked, pour the soup into a tureen. Add the *pistou,* stir well and serve immediately, passing the cheese separately.

Serves 6   *Photograph pages 18–19*

Bourgogne

CORNIOTTES

CHEESE PASTRY "HATS"

8 oz (250 g) *fromage blanc* or ricotta cheese, drained
salt and freshly ground pepper
½ cup (4 fl oz/125 ml) heavy (double) cream or crème fraîche
7 oz (200 g) Emmenthaler cheese, freshly and coarsely grated
2 eggs
1 lb (500 g) short (shortcrust) pastry (recipe page 120)
1 egg yolk
1 tablespoon water

❧ Place cheese into a bowl and mash it with a fork, adding salt, pepper and cream. Mix well. Add the Emmenthaler and eggs and mix well.
❧ Preheat an oven to 425°F (215°C). Roll out the pastry to a thickness of ⅛ in (3 mm). Cut out 26 circles, each 4 in (10 cm) in diameter.
❧ Dip your finger in cold water and moisten edges of the first pastry circle. Place a walnut-size mound of filling in the center of the pastry and turn up the edges of the circle on three sides to make a three-cornered "hat." Press the edges of the pastry firmly together at the corners so that the filling is enclosed. Repeat with the other pastry circles, arranging the *corniottes* on two nonstick baking sheets.
❧ Beat the egg yolk and water and brush this mixture over the surface of the *corniottes*. Bake for 25 minutes or until the pastries are nicely browned. Serve hot or lukewarm.

Serves 6

Lyonnais

CERVELLE DE CANUT

HERBED CHEESE SPREAD

This is a dish traditionally served in the mâchons—*the bistros of Lyon. The name* mâchon *originally referred to a small meal that was eaten mid-morning. This dish is also known as* claqueret, *from the expression "claquer le fromage," meaning to beat or whisk the cheese.* Canut *was the name of the silk workers who for a long period represented a true gourmet tradition.*

8 oz (250 g) fresh *fromage blanc* or ricotta cheese
¼ cup (2 fl oz/60 ml) olive oil
3 tablespoons white wine vinegar
3 tablespoons dry white wine
¾ cup (6 fl oz/200 ml) chilled cream
2 French shallots, finely chopped
6 sprigs flat-leaf parsley, leaves only, finely chopped
6 sprigs chervil, leaves only, finely chopped
10 chive stalks, finely chopped
salt and freshly ground pepper
whole-grain country bread or rye bread

❧ Set the cheese to drain, in the container or a colander, 12 hours before commencing preparations. Turn the drained cheese into a bowl and mash with a fork. Mix in the oil, vinegar and wine.
❧ Whip the cream until stiff and fold into the cheese mixture. Mix in the shallots, herbs, salt and pepper. Chill thoroughly and serve with the bread.

Serves 6

CHEESE PASTRY "HATS" (LEFT) AND
HERBED CHEESE SPREAD (RIGHT)

Côte d'Azur

PISSALADIÈRE

PISSALADIÈRE

The name comes from the Niçoise dialect word pissalat *meaning a purée of anchovies flavored with thyme, cloves, fennel and a dash of olive oil. But this remains strictly a local combination and is usually replaced by anchovy fillets.*

5 tablespoons (3 fl oz/80 ml) extra virgin
    olive oil
4 lb (2 kg) large onions, thinly sliced
4 cloves fresh, young garlic, finely chopped
2 tablespoons water
salt
13 oz (400 g) bread dough (recipe page 121)
16 anchovy fillets in olive oil
4 oz (125 g) black Niçoise olives, pitted

❧ Heat 4 tablespoons olive oil in a nonstick 10-in (26-cm) skillet. Add the onions and garlic and cook, stirring, over low heat for 10 minutes or until the onions are golden. Add the water and season with salt. Cover and cook gently for 30 minutes or until the onions are transparent and very soft, adding a little more water if necessary during cooking.
❧ Preheat an oven to 425°F (215°C). Lightly oil a 14- by 9-in (35- by 22-cm) baking sheet or a 12-in (30-cm) round tart pan. Gently roll out the bread dough to fit and lay it in the pan. Spread the cooked onion mixture on the surface. Arrange the anchovy fillets in a lattice pattern on top, placing an olive in the center of each square. Sprinkle with the remaining oil. Bake for 30 minutes or until the crust is golden. Serve hot or warm.

Serves 6

Val de Loire

TOURTE AUX HERBES

HERB PIE

This is a specialty of Tours.

1 lb (500 g) fresh spinach
8 oz (250 g) sorrel
8 oz (250 g) beet greens or spinach
1 lettuce heart
¼ cup (2 oz/60 g) butter
salt and freshly ground pepper
1 lb (500 g) boiling potatoes
4 sprigs parsley
4 sprigs tarragon
2 cloves garlic, finely chopped
1 lb (500 g) puff pastry (recipe page 122)
1 egg yolk
1 tablespoon water
1 cup (8 fl oz/250 ml) heavy (double) cream
    or crème fraîche

❧ Wash the spinach and sorrel and trim the stalks; drain. Wash and drain the beet greens and lettuce. Coarsely chop all four greens.
❧ Melt half the butter in a nonstick 10-in (26-cm) skillet and gradually add the greens. Season with salt and pepper and cook over high heat, stirring constantly, for 5 minutes or until all liquid has evaporated. Turn greens out onto a plate and set aside.
❧ Peel and wash the potatoes, pat dry and slice into ¼-in (5-mm) rounds. Rinse and dry the skillet. Melt the remaining butter in the skillet, add the potato and cook, turning often, for 15 minutes or until golden.
❧ Finely chop the parsley and tarragon leaves. Add the herbs and garlic to the potatoes, season with salt and pepper and cook, stirring, for 2 minutes. Remove from heat.

❧ Preheat an oven to 425°F̃ (215°C). Divide the pastry into two portions, ⅔ and ⅓. Roll out the larger portion into a 12- by 6-in (30- by 15-cm) rectangle and transfer it to a greased baking sheet. Spread half the potato mixture on the pastry to within 1 in (2 cm) of the edges. Cover with half the greens mixture, then the remaining potatoes and finally the remaining greens mixture. Roll out the remaining pastry into a 12½- by 6¾-in (32- by 17-cm) rectangle and place it over the filling. Press the two edges of the pastry together to seal.

❧ Beat the egg yolk and water with a fork in a small bowl. Brush this mixture over the entire surface of the pastry, using a pastry brush. Cut two small holes in the center of the pastry lid and insert small "chimneys" of aluminum foil or waxed paper to keep them open. Bake the pie for 45 minutes or until the pastry is golden brown.

❧ Meanwhile, season the cream with salt and pepper. When the pie is baked, pour in the cream through the two chimneys. Let rest for 10 minutes before serving.

Serves 6

Lyonnais

TÂTRE DES ALLYMES
ALLYMES TART

The tâtre *(a regional word for tart) is a specialty of the village of Allymes. It may also be made with* pâte brisée.

2 tablespoons peanut oil
1 lb (500 g) large onions, thinly sliced
4 oz (125 g) well-drained *fromage blanc* or ricotta cheese

salt and freshly ground pepper
4 pinches freshly grated nutmeg
½ cup (4 fl oz/125 ml) heavy (double) cream or crème fraîche
2 eggs
13 oz (400 g) bread dough (recipe page 121)

❧ Heat the oil in a nonstick 10-in (26-cm) skillet. Add the onions and cook, stirring, over low heat for 10 minutes or until golden.

❧ Beat the cheese in a bowl with a fork, adding salt, pepper, nutmeg and cream. Break the eggs into a separate bowl and beat with a fork until blended, then add to the cheese mixture and beat until smooth. Stir in the onions.

❧ Preheat an oven to 425°F (215°C). Lightly oil a 16- by 9-in (35- by 22-cm) baking sheet. Roll out the bread dough to the same size and lift the dough onto the sheet. Spread the onion mixture over the dough. Bake for 30 minutes or until lightly browned. Serve hot.

Serves 6

PISSALADIÈRE (TOP), ALLYMES TART (BOTTOM LEFT) AND HERB PIE (BOTTOM RIGHT)

PETITS FARCIS PROVENÇAUX
STUFFED VEGETABLES OF PROVENCE

3 eggplants (aubergines), 7 oz (200 g) each

3 zucchini (courgettes), 3 oz (100 g) each

6 firm-ripe tomatoes, 5 oz (150 g) each

6 onions, 3 oz (100 g) each

salt and freshly ground pepper

3 tablespoons extra virgin olive oil

2 cloves garlic, finely chopped

1 lb (500 g) boneless veal from the neck or
   shoulder, trimmed of fat and finely
   chopped

3 oz (100 g) fresh pork belly, finely chopped

10 sprigs flat-leaf parsley, stemmed and
   chopped

3 tablespoons boiled rice

½ cup (2 oz/50 g) freshly and finely grated
   Parmesan cheese

2 eggs

2 sprigs thyme

❧ Wash the eggplants and zucchini and pat dry. Cut in half lengthwise and remove most of the flesh, leaving ¼ in (5 mm) next to the skin. Cut off the top quarter of each tomato and hollow out the inside with a small spoon. Peel the onions, cut off the top quarter and scoop out a hollow in the center. Season the insides of all the vegetables with salt and pepper and brush lightly with oil. With a sharp knife, finely chop the flesh removed from the vegetables.

❧ Heat 1 tablespoon oil in a nonstick 10-in (26-cm) skillet. Add the garlic, chopped vegetables and meat and cook, stirring, over moderate heat for 5 minutes or until lightly browned. Transfer to a bowl and let cool.

❧ Preheat an oven to 400°F (200°C). Using 1 teaspoon oil, brush the inside of a shallow baking dish large enough to hold all the vegetables side by side.

❧ Add the parsley to the bowl with the rice, Parmesan, eggs, thyme, salt and pepper and

ANCHOVY SPREAD (TOP, RECIPE PAGE 12), NIÇOISE SALAD (BOTTOM LEFT, RECIPE PAGE 21), VEGETABLE SOUP WITH BASIL-GARLIC PASTE (CENTER, RECIPE PAGE 13) AND STUFFED VEGETABLES OF PROVENCE (BOTTOM RIGHT)

mix well. Divide the filling among the vegetables and arrange them in the prepared dish. Sprinkle with the remaining oil and pour ¼ cup (2 fl oz/60 ml) water into the dish. Bake for 45 minutes or until the vegetables are tender, basting them from time to time with the pan juices and adding a little more water if the liquid evaporates too quickly.

❧ When the vegetables are cooked, arrange them on a platter, spoon over the remaining cooking juices and serve immediately.

Serves 6

RAVIOLI

Corse / Côte d'Azur

RAVIOLIS

RAVIOLI

Traditionally, the filling for this ravioli is prepared from leftover daube *(beef stewed in tomato sauce). It can also be made with veal that has been browned briefly in oil and ground.*

FOR THE PASTA:
2 cups (10 oz/300 g) all-purpose (plain) flour
4 pinches salt
2 eggs
2 tablespoons olive oil

FOR THE FILLING:
1½ lb (750 g) cooked beef, finely chopped
1 egg
½ cup (2 oz/50 g) freshly and finely grated
    Parmesan cheese
1 lb (500 g) beet greens, Swiss chard or spinach
salt and freshly ground pepper

FOR SERVING:
tomato sauce
freshly and finely grated Parmesan cheese

❖ To prepare the pasta: sift the flour and salt onto a work surface. Make a well in the center and add the eggs and oil. Combine all ingredients, using the fingertips in a quick movement from the middle toward the edges. When the dough is homogeneous, knead by pushing it out and then bringing it back into a ball, working it until it is elastic and comes away from the fingers. Roll the dough into a ball, wrap in plastic and let rest for at least 30 minutes in a cool place.

❖ Meanwhile, prepare the filling: combine the meat, egg and cheese in a bowl and mix well. Drop the greens into boiling water for 30 seconds, then drain and squeeze dry. Let cool slightly, then chop finely with a sharp knife. Stir into the meat mixture with salt and pepper.

❖ Divide the pasta dough in half; roll out into equal-size rectangles. Place level teaspoons of the filling in small mounds on one rectangle, spaced 1 in (2 cm) apart. Moisten the dough between the mounds, using a pastry brush dipped in water, then cover with the second rectangle of dough. Seal the two sheets of dough together along the edges and around each mound of filling, pressing firmly. Cut out the ravioli using a sharp knife or a smooth-edged or crimped pastry wheel. Arrange the ravioli on a clean tea towel, taking care that they do not overlap.

❖ Bring a large pot of water to boil. Add salt, then drop in the ravioli and cook for 5 minutes. Drain and turn the ravioli into a shallow dish. Cover with tomato sauce and toss lightly, then sprinkle with a little grated Parmesan. Serve immediately, with more Parmesan offered separately.

Serves 6

Provence

SALADE NIÇOISE

NIÇOISE SALAD

This typically southern dish is made with raw vegetables, tuna, garlic, basil and olive oil. Neither cooked vegetables nor potatoes should be included.

6 eggs
1 lb (500 g) fresh broad beans
1 red bell pepper (capsicum), about 5 oz (150 g)
2 small artichokes
½ lemon
1 clove garlic
1 lb (500 g) firm-ripe tomatoes, cut into eighths
1 small cucumber, thinly sliced
3 green (spring) onions, thinly sliced
2 tender celery stalks, strings removed, cut into fine strips
12 anchovy fillets in olive oil, halved lengthwise
1 can (6½ oz/195 g) tuna in olive oil, drained and coarsely flaked
2 oz (50 g) black Niçoise olives
12 large basil leaves
salt
6 tablespoons (3 fl oz/90 ml) extra virgin olive oil

✤ Place the eggs in a saucepan of cold water, bring to boil over low heat and simmer for 10 minutes. Drain the eggs and cool under running water. Shell them and cut into quarters.
✤ Shell the broad beans and remove the green outer skins. Halve the red pepper and remove the stem, seeds and white ribs, then slice the pepper into fine slivers. Remove the outer leaves of the artichokes and trim the points of the remaining leaves. Cut each artichoke into quarters and rub the surfaces with lemon.
✤ Rub a shallow bowl with the peeled clove of garlic. Arrange in it the tomatoes, pepper, cucumber, artichokes, onions, celery and broad beans. Garnish with anchovies, tuna, olives and hard-cooked eggs. Using scissors, snip the basil leaves over the salad. Sprinkle lightly with salt. Drizzle with olive oil and serve immediately.

Serves 6 *Photograph pages 18–19*

Flandres

SOUPE DE POTIRON

PUMPKIN SOUP

3 tablespoons butter
4 leeks, white parts only, washed and thinly sliced
1½ lb (750 g) peeled pumpkin, cut into 1-in (2-cm) cubes
3 cups (24 fl oz/750 ml) chicken stock (recipe page 120)
salt and freshly ground pepper
1 cup (8 fl oz/250 ml) milk

✤ Melt half the butter in a heavy 4-qt (4-l) saucepan and cook the leeks until soft and golden, about 5 minutes, stirring constantly with a wooden spoon. Stir in the pumpkin cubes, stock, salt and pepper and simmer for about 30 minutes, until pumpkin is very soft.
✤ Transfer the mixture to a food processor and blend to a smooth purée. Reheat gently, adding the remaining butter and the milk. Stir well and remove from heat. Pour the soup into a tureen and serve immediately.

Serves 6 *Photograph page 10*

Bourgogne

OEUFS EN MEURETTE
POACHED EGGS WITH RED WINE SAUCE

The term meurette *in Bourgogne applies to any preparation based on red wine, whether it is for use with fish, meat or eggs.*

2 cups (16 fl oz/500 ml) red Burgundy
3 French shallots, finely chopped
2 carrots, peeled and finely chopped
⅔ cup (5 oz/150 g) butter, cut into small pieces
1¼ cups (10 fl oz/300 ml) red wine vinegar
12 eggs
salt and freshly ground pepper

❧ Pour the wine into a nonaluminum sauce-pan, add the shallots and carrots and boil over high heat for 5 minutes to reduce.
❧ Reduce heat to very low and whisk in the pieces of butter one or two at a time. Strain the sauce into a small saucepan and keep warm over hot water.
❧ Combine 2 qt (2 l) water and the vinegar in a skillet and bring to a gentle simmer. Break the eggs into a bowl, one after the other. As soon as the water begins to bubble, delicately slide in the eggs. Carefully turn the eggs over with a skimming spoon to bring the white over the yolk. Poach for 4 minutes.
❧ When the eggs are cooked, remove them with the skimming spoon and transfer to a clean cloth. Trim the ragged edges of each egg to give a nice oval shape. Divide the sauce among six warm plates and arrange 2 eggs in the middle of each. Season with salt and pepper and serve immediately.

Serves 6

Bourgogne

JAMBON PERSILLÉ
PARSLEYED HAM

This is the traditional Easter Sunday dish in Bourgogne.

2 lb (1 kg) unsmoked raw ham
2 calf's feet
10-oz (300-g) veal knuckle
2 French shallots, halved
1 clove garlic, halved
1 sprig dried thyme
1 bay leaf
2 sprigs tarragon
3 sprigs chervil
10 sprigs flat-leaf parsley
salt and freshly ground pepper
3 cups (24 fl oz/750 ml) white Burgundy
2 tablespoons white wine vinegar

❧ In a large bowl, cover the ham with cold water and let soak for 12 hours to remove the excess salt.
❧ Blanch the calf's feet in boiling water to cover for 5 minutes, then drain. Drain the ham and rinse under running water. Combine the calf's feet, ham and veal knuckle in a large pot; add the shallots, garlic, thyme, bay leaf, tarragon, chervil and 3 sprigs of parsley. Season lightly with salt and pepper, and pour in the wine. Bring to boil over gentle heat and simmer for 2 hours, stirring occasionally.
❧ Snip the leaves from the remaining parsley. Drain the ham and the veal knuckle meat and crush the meat with a fork. Strain the cooking liquid and stir in salt, pepper and vinegar. Let cool until the stock is thick and viscous.

POACHED EGGS WITH RED WINE SAUCE (LEFT) AND PARSLEYED HAM (RIGHT)

✤ Pour a layer of the stock into a mold just large enough to accommodate the meat and liquid. Let cool, then refrigerate until firmly set. Cover with a layer of meat, then sprinkle with parsley. Pour more stock over and again refrigerate to set. Repeat the layers until all ingredients have been used, ending with a layer of stock. Cover the mold and refrigerate for 12 hours before unmolding. Serve in slices, accompanied by salad.

Serves 8

SHELLFISH OF THE SEA AND RIVERS

OYSTERS FROM CANCALE, from the bay of Morbihan, from Belon, from Saint-Vaast-la Hougue, from Marennes-Oléron: each has its own distinctive flavor. Today, the oyster is firmly established in French cuisine, and even dieters appreciate it.

Mussels are generally cultivated on fixed wooden stakes in the waters off Oléron and La Rochelle; these are the best. Others are grown in special "parks" at Croisic or, in the Mediterranean, on ropes. Their tender, flavorful flesh lends itself to many cooking variations: *marinière* style, in the preparation known as *éclade,* where a quick fire directly on top of the mussels causes them to open, or *mouclade,* a mussel stew with white wine and cream.

Scallops, firm-fleshed and delicate, and their baby sisters the *pétoncles,* white-fleshed mollusks with an almost-sweet flavor, can take only a very brief cooking, which preserves their iodine and their savor.

Lobster and crayfish, which are the kings of the Breton coasts, are served grilled, with *beurre blanc* sauce. Spices and strongly flavored sauces should be used sparingly.

Shrimp—the tiny ones, *grises,* and the larger ones, *bouquets*—make excellent first courses. Langoustines, which resemble baby lobsters in shape, are easily cooked—but watch the time! A few seconds too long, and a firm, crisp-textured flesh becomes soft and stringy. Only the tail is used, pan-fried.

There is a whole family of crabs, all hiding soft, pinkish flesh under a hard red shell. The *tourteau* (common crab) is the most hardy; the *étrille* (swimmer) is smaller and more delicate; the *araignée* (spider crab) is the rarest and tastiest. All are rich in vitamins, low in calories and exquisite served cold with a lemony mayonnaise.

Freshwater crustaceans are gradually disappearing from French rivers as a result of pollution. The crayfish, or *écrevisses,* that were once plentiful in small streams, lakes and reservoirs, now usually come from other countries (Turkey, in particular). The most highly reputed are the *pattes rouges,* the red-legged variety.

Contrary to popular opinion, squid and small cuttlefish are not fish but mollusks. According to region, they may be stuffed, cooked with sweet peppers or tomatoes, or served with a sauce, their firm flesh retaining its distinctive taste and appearance regardless of recipe.

INGREDIENTS FOR CRAYFISH IN CHAMPAGNE
(RECIPE PAGE 28)

SCALLOPS LANDES STYLE (TOP, RECIPE PAGE 33) AND SCALLOPS WITH BEURRE BLANC (BOTTOM)

(TOP, RECIPE PAGE 33)

Bretagne

COQUILLES SAINT-JACQUES AU BEURRE BLANC

SCALLOPS WITH BEURRE BLANC

Beurre blanc *sauce is a reduction of French shallots and vinegar with butter incorporated into it. In Anjou, and in the Nantes area where it is a specialty, it is made with unsalted butter, which has a delicious nutty flavor, and accompanies pike or shad. In Bretagne it is made the same way, but with a semi-salted butter that has a subtle taste of iodine and is used to coat crustaceans and fish.*

1 lb (500 g) scallops (without their coral)
salt and freshly ground pepper

4 French shallots, finely chopped
6 tablespoons (3 fl oz/90 ml) dry white wine
3 tablespoons white wine vinegar
¾ cup (7 oz/200 g) butter

❧ Rinse scallops and pat dry. Cut each horizontally in half, making 2 thinner discs. Season with salt and pepper. Combine the shallots, wine, vinegar and salt and pepper in a small saucepan. Simmer gently over low heat until only 2 teaspoons of liquid remain.
❧ Meanwhile, cut the butter into ¾-in (1.5-cm) cubes; set aside 1½ tablespoons. Over a very low heat, vigorously whisk the butter into the saucepan, piece by piece.

When all the butter has been incorporated and the *beurre blanc* is light and foamy, set it aside and keep warm.

❧ Melt the remaining butter in a nonstick 10-in (26-cm) skillet and cook the scallops over very low heat for 20 seconds on each side. Divide among four hot plates and pour the sauce over. Serve immediately.

Serves 4

Limousin

LIMOUSINE D'ÉCREVISSES
CRAYFISH LIMOUSIN STYLE

24 live crayfish (small yabbies)
2 tablespoons butter
2 French shallots, finely chopped
salt and freshly ground pepper
2 tablespoons cognac
2 cups (16 fl oz/500 ml) dry white wine
3 tablespoons tomato paste (purée), optional
bouquet garni: 1 bay leaf, 1 sprig thyme,
    6 sprigs parsley (tied together)
6 tablespoons (3 fl oz/90 ml) heavy (double)
    cream or crème fraîche
2 egg yolks
2 pinches cayenne pepper
2 tablespoons chopped fresh tarragon

❧ To prepare the crayfish: lift up the central tail fin and twist it to remove the small black vein that runs through the center of the tail. Rinse and drain the crayfish.

❧ Melt the butter in a nonstick 11-in (28-cm) sauté pan. Add the crayfish, cover and cook for 5 minutes. Add the shallots, season with salt and pepper and cook, stirring, over low heat for 2 minutes. Pour in the cognac and ignite, shaking the pan gently until flames subside. Add the wine, tomato paste and bouquet garni and cook over high heat, stirring, for 2 minutes. Remove the crayfish with a slotted spoon and keep warm.

❧ Boil the cooking liquid until syrupy, about 5 minutes. Add half the cream and cook for 2 more minutes. Remove the bouquet garni.

❧ Beat the egg yolks with a fork; beat in the remaining cream. Pour into the sauté pan and remove from heat; stir with a wooden spoon until the sauce is smooth and thickened. Add the crayfish and cayenne and reheat, stirring, for 30 seconds.

❧ Turn the crayfish and sauce onto a large platter, sprinkle with chopped tarragon and serve immediately.

Serves 4

CRAYFISH LIMOUSIN STYLE

Champagne

ÉCREVISSES AU CHAMPAGNE
CRAYFISH IN CHAMPAGNE

36 live crayfish (small yabbies)
3 tablespoons butter
3 French shallots, finely chopped
salt and freshly ground pepper
1 tablespoon *marc de champagne* or
    cognac
¾ cup (6 fl oz/200 ml) dry champagne
¾ cup (6 fl oz/200 ml) heavy (double) cream
    or crème fraîche
2 pinches cayenne pepper
1 tablespoon chopped fresh tarragon

❧ To prepare the crayfish: lift up the central tail fin and twist it to remove the small black vein that runs through the center of the tail. Rinse and drain the crayfish.

❧ Melt the butter in a 10-in (26-cm) sauté pan. Add the shallots and cook, stirring, for 3 minutes or until softened. Add the crayfish and cook for 5 minutes, stirring constantly. Season with salt and pepper, then pour in the *marc* and ignite, shaking the pan gently until flames subside. Add the champagne, bring to boil, cover and simmer for 5 minutes.

❧ Transfer the crayfish to a serving platter with a slotted spoon and keep warm. Boil the cooking liquid over high heat until reduced by half. Stir in the cream and cook over high heat for 2–3 minutes or until the sauce is slightly thickened. Season sauce with cayenne pepper and strain over the crayfish. Sprinkle with chopped tarragon and serve immediately.

Serves 4   *Photograph page 24*

Pays Basque

ARAIGNÉE FARCIE
STUFFED SPIDER CRAB

2 tablespoons coarse sea salt
4 live spider (blue swimmer) crabs, about
    1½ lb (800 g) each
1 lb (500 g) ripe tomatoes
2 tablespoons vegetable oil
1 onion, finely chopped
1 leek, white part only, washed and finely
    chopped
2 French shallots, finely chopped
1 carrot, peeled and finely chopped
1 tender celery stalk with leaves, finely chopped
1 fresh chili pepper, finely chopped
3 tablespoons dry sherry
6 tablespoons (3 fl oz/90 ml) chicken stock
    (recipe page 120)
salt and freshly ground pepper
1 tablespoon chopped flat-leaf parsley
1 tablespoon dry breadcrumbs
1 tablespoon freshly and finely grated
    Parmesan cheese

❧ In a large pot, bring 3 qt (3 l) water to boil. Add the sea salt, plunge in the spider crabs and return to boil, then cook 15 minutes.

❧ Drop the tomatoes into a separate pot of boiling water for 10 seconds, then cool under running water. Peel, halve and squeeze out the seeds; chop the flesh finely.

❧ Drain the cooked crabs and let cool, then shell. Roughly shred and set aside the meat, the coral and the creamy parts from the shell. Scrub the shells under running water; set aside.

❧ Preheat an oven to 450°F (230°C). Heat the oil in a nonstick 10-in (26-cm) sauté pan.

STUFFED SPIDER CRAB

Add the chopped vegetables and cook, stirring, over moderate heat for 5 minutes or until golden. Add the sherry and cook until evaporated, stirring constantly. Stir in the tomatoes and chicken stock; season with salt and pepper. Cook over high heat until all liquid is evaporated, about 5 minutes. Add the crab mixture and cook, stirring, for 2 minutes. Remove from heat and stir in the parsley.

✤ Divide the filling among the crab shells. Combine the breadcrumbs and cheese and sprinkle over the surface. Bake until lightly browned, about 15 minutes. Serve hot.

Serves 4

Normandie / Bretagne

MOULES MARINIÈRE

MUSSELS IN WHITE WINE

This is a traditional dish served all over France. It is usually made with a local white wine.

6 lb (3 kg) mussels
3 tablespoons butter

6 French shallots, finely chopped
1 clove garlic, finely chopped
2 cups (16 fl oz/500 ml) dry white wine such as muscadet
bouquet garni: 1 bay leaf, 1 sprig thyme, 6 sprigs parsley (tied together)
freshly ground pepper
2 tablespoons chopped flat-leaf parsley

MUSSELS IN WHITE WINE

❧ Scrape the mussels and remove the beards. Wash in several changes of water and drain.

❧ Melt the butter in a saucepan large enough to hold all the mussels. Add the chopped shallots and garlic and cook over low heat, stirring, for 1 minute or until softened. Pour in the wine, add the bouquet garni and season with pepper; bring to boil. Boil for 2 minutes, then add the mussels and stir with a slotted spoon. As soon as they open, remove them with the slotted spoon and keep warm in a large bowl. Discard any unopened mussels.

❧ Boil the cooking liquid over high heat until reduced by half, then return the mussels to the pan and add the chopped parsley. Mix all together just long enough to reheat the mussels, about 30 seconds. Remove the bouquet garni.

❧ Divide the mussels and liquid among four large shallow soup bowls and serve immediately.

Serves 4

Normandie

COQUILLES SAINT-JACQUES D'ÉTRETAT

SCALLOPS ÉTRETAT STYLE

With its shingle and tall cliffs making it one of Normandie's prettiest "postcards," Étretat is also a gastronomic mecca, famous for its shellfish and crustaceans.

1 lb (500 g) scallops, with their coral
salt and freshly ground pepper
8 oz (250 g) mushrooms
6 tablespoons (3 fl oz/90 ml) heavy (double) cream or crème fraîche
2 egg yolks
3 tablespoons butter
2 French shallots, finely chopped
1 tablespoon *calvados*
1 cup (8 fl oz/250 ml) dry white wine

❧ Rinse the scallops and coral and pat dry. Season with salt and pepper. Trim the stems of the mushrooms; wash them, pat dry and chop finely. Beat the cream and egg yolks together with a fork in a small bowl.

❧ Melt the butter in a nonstick 10-in (26-cm) skillet and cook the chopped shallots and mushrooms over very low heat, stirring, for 5 minutes. Add the scallops and coral and cook for 30 seconds on each side. Sprinkle in the *calvados* and ignite, shaking the pan gently until flames subside. Remove the scallops and set aside in a warm place.

❧ Pour the wine into the skillet and boil over high heat until the sauce is syrupy and reduced by ⅔. Add the egg yolk mixture and stir until the sauce thickens; do not allow it to boil.

❧ Preheat a broiler (griller). Divide the scallops among four individual broilerproof dishes and cover with sauce. Slide under the broiler, close to the heat source, for about 30 seconds or until lightly browned. Serve immediately in the same dishes.

Serves 4

Photograph page 32

Normandie

MOULES À LA CRÈME
MUSSELS IN CREAM

Mussels are cultivated in different ways in different regions. The best known are those grown in Charentes on wooden stakes, or bouchots, *to which they attach themselves in clusters. In Bretagne mussels are cultivated like oysters—flat, in beds. In the south they are grown hanging, and in the Etang de Thau the famous Bouzigues mussels live permanently submerged, but without contact with the bottom of the lagoon.*

8 lb (4 kg) mussels
2 cups (16 fl oz/500 ml) dry cider
4 French shallots, finely chopped
¾ cup (6 fl oz/185 ml) heavy (double) cream
   or crème fraîche
salt and freshly ground pepper
3 egg yolks
1 tablespoon chopped parsley

❖ Scrape the mussels and remove the beards. Wash in several changes of water and drain.
❖ Pour the cider into a pot large enough to hold the mussels and place over high heat. Add the shallots and boil for 2 minutes. Add the mussels and stir with a slotted spoon. As soon as they open, remove the mussels with the slotted spoon and keep warm in a large bowl.
❖ Pour half the cream into the pot and cook over high heat until the sauce is smooth and slightly thickened. Strain into a small saucepan and keep warm. Season with salt and pepper.
❖ Beat together the remaining cream and the egg yolks with a fork. Pour this mixture into the small saucepan and whisk over low heat until the sauce becomes thick and creamy; take care that the sauce does not boil and become grainy. Stir in the parsley. Divide the mussels among four warm plates and pour the sauce over. Serve immediately.

Serves 4

Aquitaine

COQUILLES SAINT-JACQUES À LA LANDAISE
SCALLOPS LANDES STYLE

⅓ cup (2 oz/50 g) pine nuts
1 lb (500 g) scallops, with their coral
salt and freshly ground pepper
2 tablespoons vegetable oil
1 tablespoon wine vinegar
1 tablespoon water
3 tablespoons butter
1 tablespoon chopped flat-leaf parsley

❖ Lightly brown the pine nuts over low heat in a dry skillet. Set aside in a bowl.
❖ Rinse the scallops and pat dry. Cut the white parts horizontally in half making two thin discs; season both the white parts and the coral with salt and pepper.
❖ Heat the oil in a nonstick 10-in (26-cm) skillet. Lightly brown the scallops and coral over moderate heat for 1 minute on each side. Set aside and keep warm.
❖ Discard the cooking oil. Add the vinegar and water to the pan and boil until reduced by half. Add the butter and whisk over low heat until it softens and becomes incorporated into the sauce. Add the parsley and pine nuts and stir again. Pour this sauce over the scallops and serve immediately.

Serves 4   *Photograph page 26*

Provence

CALMARS AU RIZ
SQUID WITH RICE

The name calmar *comes from the old French* calamar, *an eighteenth-century word for a desk. Like a desk, squid contains all that is necessary for writing: ink and a pen (the name given to its small transparent bone).*

2½ lb (1.2 kg) medium squid
8 oz (250 g) ripe tomatoes
2 onions, finely chopped
3 cloves garlic, finely chopped
3 tablespoons olive oil
4 pinches saffron threads
1 teaspoon *herbes de Provence* (see glossary)
1 teaspoon fennel seeds
salt and freshly ground pepper
2 pinches cayenne pepper
1½ cups (10 oz/300 g) Camargue
   (long-grain) rice
3 cups (24 fl oz/750 ml) water

❧ Place one squid on a work surface. Hold the body with one hand and pull away the tentacles with the other. Discard the insides and the internal quill. Cut the tentacles off the head at the level of the eyes and reserve, discarding the rest of the head. Wash the tentacles and body; if the latter contains eggs or roe, leave them, as they have an excellent flavor. Cut both the tentacles and the body into ⅜-in (1-cm) crosswise slices. Prepare the remaining squid in the same way.

❧ Drop the tomatoes into boiling water for 10 seconds. Cool under running water, then peel, halve and squeeze out seeds; chop flesh finely.

❧ Cook the squid in a 6-qt (6-l) enameled pot over low heat, stirring with a wooden spoon, until they give out no more liquid. Add the chopped onions and garlic, stir again and cook until no more liquid remains. Add the oil, saffron, herbs, fennel seed, salt, pepper, cayenne and rice and cook, stirring, until everything is lightly browned.

❧ Add the tomatoes and water to the pot and bring to boil. Cover and cook until the rice is tender, about 25 minutes. Serve hot, directly from the pot.

Serves 6

Provence

LES BAISERS
KISSES

The Provençal name for these is lei poutoun. *The delicious kissing sounds made by the diners as they savor this dish give it its name.*

FOR THE *AÏOLI:*
1 clove garlic, coarsely chopped
1 egg yolk
2 pinches salt
3 tablespoons peanut oil
3 tablespoons olive oil

FOR THE CLAMS:
4 lb (2 kg) fresh spinach
1 tablespoon olive oil
1 onion, finely chopped
salt
4 lb (2 kg) clams

❧ To prepare the *aïoli:* combine the garlic, egg yolk and salt in a blender or food processor

KISSES (FRONT) AND SQUID WITH RICE (REAR), PHOTOGRAPHED IN PROVENCE

and mix for 10 seconds. With machine running, pour in the peanut oil and then the olive oil, blending until thick. Set aside.

⚜ Trim the stalks from the spinach; wash and drain the leaves. Cut the leaves into strips ⅜ in (1 cm) wide.

⚜ Heat oil in a large nonstick sauté pan. Add the onion and cook over low heat, stirring, for 3 minutes or until golden. Add the spinach and season with salt. Mix well and cook, covered, for 5 minutes or until the spinach is very soft.

⚜ Wash the clams in several changes of water; drain. Transfer to a large pot and cook over high heat, turning constantly, until all have opened. Discard any unopened clams. Remove the clams with a slotted spoon and keep warm; discard the shells.

⚜ Strain the clam cooking liquid into a small saucepan and boil until reduced by half. Blend into the *aïoli*. Turn this mixture into the spinach and stir well. Add the clams, stir and serve immediately.

Serves 4

FISH

From Dunkirk to Menton, France has four coasts: on the North Sea, the Channel, the Atlantic Ocean and the Mediterranean. This last-mentioned, tideless, has seen its catches diminish. In the north, however, the herring and mackerel that are the mainstay of the port of Boulogne are still plentiful. They are smoked immediately, in the port, before being exported to all parts of the globe. Sardines, which do very nicely in Brittany, are the success story of the port of Quiberon. An abundance of tuna is fished at Saint-Jean-de-Luz, in the Basque country, and anchovies are the pride of Collioure, on the Mediterranean close to the border.

Although they still form the basis of some superb regional dishes, these are popular, everyday fish rather than gourmet specialties. Simple treatments—pan-frying, grilling, steaming and oven-baking—are often sympathetically paired with flavored butters, or vegetable-based sauces, or a reduced fish stock *(fumet)*.

Each region complements its fish with its own particular flavors: peppers in the south; cider in Normandy; muscadet in the region of Nantes; garlic around Nice and in Provence; a Riesling sauce in Alsace; aromatic fennel around the Mediterranean, as in the classic grilled bass. And of course it should be remembered that the hazards of geography change the names of some fish.

After leaving the shores of the Mediterranean, sea bass is no longer *loup* but *bar* in the ocean and *louvine* in the Gulf of Gascony. Similarly, the *baudroie* or anglerfish of the southern coasts becomes the *lotte* of the north.

The *caudière berckoise,* prepared in the north between Berk-Plage and Dunkirk, is enriched with potatoes, onions, white wine, garlic and cream. *Ttoro,* the soup of the fishermen of Saint-Jean-de-Luz, combines oil, pimiento, tomatoes and small red peppers in the Basque style. The *chaudrée* of Aunis and Saintonge, prepared in Charentes, combines eel with fish from the sea and local butter. Potatoes turn up again in the Breton *cotriade* in company with sorrel, butter and vinegar. These are four different versions of one dish in which the sea and the coast marry with the countryside of the immediate hinterland.

The Loire salmon are surrounded by an almost mythical aura. Their delicate pink flesh is best accompanied by butter flavored with shallot, vinegar and white wine—the celebrated *beurre blanc* or *beurre nantais,* which pairs equally well with turbot and pike.

If the pike and perch often come from Holland, the carp, which enter into Jewish cuisine either cold or stuffed, are reappearing in the lakes of Berry and in Alsace, where they are simply fried, and in Sologne, where it is customary to cook them with red wine and small cubes of salt pork.

BOURRIDE (LEFT, RECIPE PAGE 48) AND BOUILLABAISSE (RIGHT, RECIPE PAGE 39), PHOTOGRAPHED IN PROVENCE

SOLE MEUNIÈRE

Bretagne

SOLE MEUNIÈRE

SOLE MEUNIÈRE

Before the days of nonstick pans, fish had to be floured before being pan-fried in butter, which accounts for the origin of the name of this dish (la meunière is a miller's wife or female owner of a flour mill). The name still applies to any fish cooked in butter.

4 sole, about 6 oz (200 g) each
salt and freshly ground pepper
⅔ cup (5 oz/150 g) salted butter
1 tablespoon fresh lemon juice
2 tablespoons chopped flat-leaf parsley

❧ Ask the fishmonger to clean and skin the sole. Rinse them and pat dry. Season with salt and pepper.

❧ Using two nonstick 10-in (26-cm) skillets, melt half the butter and cook the sole for 4 minutes on each side. Transfer them to 4 heated plates. Discard the cooking butter in one of the skillets and add the remaining butter. Add the lemon juice and let the butter melt over very low heat. Pour this sauce over the sole, sprinkle with parsley and serve immediately.

Serves 4

Provence

BOUILLABAISSE

BOUILLABAISSE

Bouillabaisse was invented by Mediterranean fishermen who, when they returned from a fishing trip, would cook their more modest fish with a few shellfish in a huge cauldron over a wood fire using olive oil, a piece of dried orange peel and some saffron. Gradually it became a highlight of the cuisine of the Midi region, each cook adding his or her own individual touch.

6 lb (3 kg) of a mixture of fish and crustaceans: rock cod, John Dory, monkfish (anglerfish), blue-eye cod, eel, sea bass, snapper, red mullet, cuttlefish, sole, brill (Petrale sole), small crabs, lobster, crayfish . . .

¼ cup (2 fl oz/60 ml) extra virgin olive oil

1 lb (500 g) ripe tomatoes, coarsely chopped

2 carrots, peeled and thinly sliced

1 leek, well washed and thinly sliced

1 celery stalk, thinly sliced

1 onion, thinly sliced

1 sprig dried thyme

1 sprig dried rosemary

1 sprig dried fennel

1 bay leaf

1 strip dried orange peel

10 cloves garlic

10 sprigs parsley

6 pinches saffron threads

salt and freshly ground pepper

2 cups (16 fl oz/500 ml) dry white wine

FOR SERVING:

slices of toasted baguette (French bread)

cloves of garlic, halved

❦ Ask the fishmonger to scale and gut the fish and remove the heads. Reserve the heads, bones and shells. Cut the large fish into 1½-in (4-cm) chunks and leave the others whole. Wash all the fish and pat dry. If crayfish or lobster is included, cut it in half to separate the head from the tail and remove the grainy sac from the head. Clean the cuttlefish, keeping only the body and tentacles; wash and pat dry.

❦ Heat the oil in a 6-qt (6-l) saucepan. Add the heads, bones and shells of the fish and crustaceans and cook over low heat, stirring, for 5 minutes. Add the tomatoes, carrots, leek, celery and onion and cook, stirring, for 5 minutes or until the vegetables are lightly colored. Add the thyme, rosemary, fennel, bay leaf, orange peel, garlic, parsley, saffron, salt and pepper and stir for 1 minute. Add the wine and simmer gently for 45 minutes.

❦ Remove the fish trimmings, thyme, rosemary, fennel, bay leaf, orange peel, garlic and parsley. Purée the tomato mixture in a blender or food processor until smooth.

❦ Wipe the saucepan and return the puréed mixture to it. Bring to boil over low heat. Add the fish, beginning with those with the firmest flesh (cuttlefish, eel, monkfish, rock cod, red mullet) and later adding those with softer flesh (John Dory, sea bass, sole, brill), letting the mixture return to boil between additions. Finally add the crustaceans. Simmer for 10 minutes, remove seafood with a slotted spoon and arrange on a plate. Keep warm.

❦ Pour the soup into a tureen and serve hot, over slices of bread rubbed with garlic. Follow with the seafood as a separate course.

Serves 6–8   *Photograph page 36*

Pays Basque

TTORO

TTORO

1 pollack or gemfish, about 2 lb (1 kg)
2 rock cod or trevally, about 1 lb (500 g) each
2 red gurnard or white-fleshed fish, about
    1 lb (500 g) each
1 lb (500 g) monkfish (anglerfish) or
    blue-eye cod
8 oz (250 g) mussels
6 uncooked langoustines (Dublin Bay prawns)
    or crayfish (yabbies)
6 tablespoons (3 fl oz/90 ml) extra virgin
    olive oil
2 cloves garlic, halved
1 small fresh chili pepper, seeded and chopped
1 onion, thinly sliced
8 oz (250 g) ripe tomatoes, coarsely chopped
1 sprig thyme
1 bay leaf
2 cups (16 fl oz/500 ml) dry white wine
salt and freshly ground pepper
croutons
cloves of garlic, halved

❧ Ask the fishmonger to scale and gut the fish and remove the heads. Reserve the heads and bones. Cut the monkfish into ¾-in (2-cm) slices, and the others into 1½-in (4-cm) chunks.

❧ Scrub the mussels in several changes of water and remove the beards. Drain well. Rinse the langoustines.

❧ Heat half the oil in an enameled 4-qt (4-l) pot. Add the fish heads and bones and cook, stirring, over low heat for 5 minutes. Add the garlic, chili and onion and cook, stirring, for 5 minutes or until the vegetables are golden.

Add the tomatoes, thyme and bay leaf and cook, stirring, for 1 minute. Pour in the wine and simmer gently for 45 minutes. Strain the liquid into a shallow baking dish.

❧ Preheat an oven to 425°F (215°C). Wipe out the pot and pour in the remaining oil. Cook the fish for 3 minutes on each side, then transfer to the baking dish. Add the langoustines and mussels and bake for 5 minutes to reheat the stock and cook the langoustines and mussels.

❧ Remove dish from the oven and serve hot, accompanied by croutons rubbed with garlic.

Serves 6   *Photograph pages 42–43*

Charentes

CHAUDRÉE

CHAUDRÉE

As popular in Charentes as the bouillabaisse is in Provence, the chaudrée contains one invariable ingredient: the white part of the squid. Sometimes it includes potatoes.

4 lb (2 kg) mixed fish: skate, sea eel, dogfish
    (rock salmon), turbot or gemfish, sole,
    blue-eye cod . . .
1 lb (500 g) cleaned squid, bodies only
salt and freshly ground pepper
4 onions, thinly sliced
8 cloves garlic
2 tablespoons oil
2 cups (16 fl oz/500 ml) dry white wine
2 cups (16 fl oz/500 ml) water
⅓ cup (3 oz/100 g) butter
croutons

❧ Ask the fishmonger to scale and gut the fish and remove the heads. Cut the large fish into 1½-in (4-cm) chunks and leave the others whole. Wash them and pat dry. Rinse the squid and pat dry; cut into strips ¾ in (2 cm) wide. Season with salt and pepper.

❧ Transfer the strips of squid to an enameled 6-qt (6-l) pot and place over low heat. Cook, stirring with a wooden spoon, until the squid have given out all their liquid. Add the onion and garlic and stir until all the liquid is absorbed. Add the oil and cook, stirring, until the squid is lightly browned all over. Pour in the wine and water and bring to simmer.

❧ Add the fish to the simmering liquid, beginning with those with the firmest flesh (skate, eel, dogfish), then adding those with softer flesh (sole, turbot) and letting the liquid return to simmer after each addition. Season with salt and pepper and simmer for 15 minutes. Add the butter to the pot and let it melt. Serve the *chaudrée* immediately, with croutons.

Serves 6   *Photograph pages 42–43*

Photograph pages 42–43

Languedoc

THON À LA LANGUEDOCIENNE
TUNA LANGUEDOC STYLE

1 slice fresh tuna, about 2½ lb (1.2 kg) and
   ¾ in (2 cm) thick
salt and freshly ground pepper
3 lemons
3 tablespoons all-purpose (plain) flour
3 tablespoons extra virgin olive oil
10 cloves garlic, peeled
2 cups (16 fl oz/500 ml) dry white wine

❧ Rinse the tuna and pat dry. Season with salt and pepper. Wash the lemons and thinly slice two of them. Squeeze 1 tablespoon of juice from the third lemon.

❧ Sprinkle the flour into a shallow bowl and coat the fish on both sides, shaking off excess.

❧ Heat the oil in a sauté pan just large enough to hold the slice of tuna. Lightly brown it for 4 minutes on each side, then remove and keep warm. Add the garlic cloves and cook until golden, about 2 minutes. Set aside with the fish. Stir the wine and lemon juice into the sauté pan and boil until reduced by half. Return the tuna and garlic to the pan and cook, covered, over low heat for 10 minutes, turning the fish after 5 minutes.

❧ Arrange the tuna and garlic on a shallow plate and keep warm. Reduce the cooking liquid over high heat to a smooth consistency and pour over the fish. Serve immediately.

Serves 6

TUNA LANGUEDOC STYLE

PHOTOGRAPHED IN PAYS BASQUE: ANCHOVIES IN TXAKOLI WINE (LEFT, RECIPE PAGE 49), MARINATED MACKEREL (CENTER FRONT),
TTORO (BOTTOM RIGHT, RECIPE PAGE 40) AND CHAUDRÉE (TOP RIGHT, RECIPE PAGE 40)

Bretagne / Charentes

MAQUEREAUX MARINÉS

MARINATED MACKEREL

Caught by the line fishermen from the Gulf of Saint-Malo to the Gulf of Gascogne, the little mackerel used in this recipe are known as lisettes.

12 small mackerel, about 3 oz (100 g) each
salt
2 cups (16 fl oz/500 ml) dry white wine
1 onion, thinly sliced
2 carrots, peeled and thinly sliced
1 lemon, cut into thin rounds
2½ tablespoons white wine vinegar
bouquet garni: 1 bay leaf, 1 sprig thyme,
    6 sprigs parsley (tied together)
2 cloves
1 teaspoon peppercorns
1 dried red chili pepper or pimiento,
    crumbled

❧ Ask the fishmonger to gut the fish; rinse them, pat dry and season with salt.

❧ Pour the wine into a 10-in (26-cm) sauté pan. Add the onion, carrots, lemon, vinegar, bouquet garni, cloves, salt, peppercorns and dried pepper. Bring to boil and simmer for 10 minutes. Add fish and simmer for 5 minutes.

❧ Remove the fish and drain well. Boil the stock until slightly reduced, about 5 more minutes. In a rectangular terrine, alternate the fish with slices of onion, carrot and lemon. Strain the stock; pour over the fish and let cool. Cover the terrine and refrigerate for 12 hours before serving.

Serves 4

Provence

LOUP AU FENOUIL
GRILLED SEA BASS WITH FENNEL

1 sea bass, snapper or silver bream, about
   3 lb (1.5 kg)
salt and freshly ground pepper
¼ cup (2 fl oz/60 ml) olive oil
10 stalks dried fennel

FOR THE SAUCE:
1 clove garlic
½ teaspoon strong mustard
1 small egg yolk
salt and pepper
6 tablespoons (3 fl oz/90 ml) extra virgin
   olive oil
1 teaspoon white wine vinegar
3 cornichons (small French sour pickles or
   gherkins), finely chopped
1 tablespoon capers, drained and finely chopped
2 tablespoons chopped flat-leaf parsley
1 tablespoon chopped chives

❧ Ask the fishmonger to scale and gut the fish; rinse it and pat dry. Season inside and out with salt and pepper. Stuff the fish with some of the dried fennel and brush the skin with olive oil.

❧ Preheat a broiler (griller). Place remaining fennel in the broiler pan, place the rack over the fennel and lay the fish on the rack. Broil for 25 minutes, turning after about 12 minutes.

❧ Meanwhile, prepare the sauce: force garlic through a press into a bowl. Add the mustard, egg yolk and salt and stir well. Set aside for 1 minute, then add the oil in a thin stream, whisking until the mixture is quite firm. Add the vinegar and whisk for 30 seconds more, then blend in the cornichons, capers, parsley and chives. Pour the sauce into a sauceboat.

❧ Arrange the cooked fish on a platter and serve immediately, passing the sauce separately.

Serves 4   *Photograph page 51*

Provence

GRATIN DE SARDINES AUX ÉPINARDS
BAKED SARDINES WITH SPINACH

1¼ lb (600 g) fresh medium sardines
2 lb (1 kg) fresh spinach
salt
1 small egg
1 oz (30 g) Emmenthaler or Parmesan cheese,
   freshly and finely grated
¼ cup (2 fl oz/60 ml) extra virgin olive oil
freshly ground pepper
½ teaspoon dried thyme
¼ cup (1 oz/30 g) dried breadcrumbs

❧ Scale the sardines and remove the heads; gut and rinse the fish. Split them along the belly and separate the two fillets, removing the row of bones beneath the dorsal fins and tail. Pat the fillets dry using paper towels.

❧ Wash and stem the spinach. Cut the leaves, with the water clinging to them, into strips ¾ in (2 cm) wide and place in a large saucepan. Season with salt and cook, covered, over high heat for 5 minutes. Drain the spinach and turn into a bowl. Beat the egg; mix in half the cheese and season with salt and pepper. Blend this mixture into the spinach.

❧ Preheat an oven to 450°F (230°C). Using some of the olive oil, lightly oil a baking dish just large enough to hold the fillets in a single layer. Spread the spinach mixture over the bottom, then arrange the sardine fillets on top, skin side down. Season with salt and pepper, sprinkle with thyme and pour the remaining oil over. Combine the breadcrumbs with the remaining cheese and sprinkle over the fish. Bake until lightly browned, about 15 minutes. Serve hot, directly from the baking dish.

Serves 4–5

BAKED SARDINES WITH SPINACH (TOP) AND STUFFED SARDINES

Provence

SARDINES FARCIES
STUFFED SARDINES

2 lb (1 kg) fresh medium sardines
salt and freshly ground pepper
8 oz (250 g) fresh spinach
¼ cup (2 fl oz/60 ml) extra virgin olive oil
2 green onions (scallions or spring onions), finely chopped
2 cloves garlic, finely chopped
1 egg
8 oz (250 g) ewe's milk cheese, *Brousse de brebis* or ricotta
2 tablespoons flat-leaf parsley, chopped
¼ cup (1 oz/30 g) dried breadcrumbs
6 pinches freshly grated nutmeg

❦ Scale the sardines and remove the heads; gut and rinse the fish. Split them along the belly and open out without separating the fillets. Remove the backbone, breaking it off at the tail. Pat the fish dry with paper towels. Season inside and out with salt and pepper.

❦ Wash and stem the spinach. Place the leaves, with the water clinging to them, in a saucepan. Season with salt and cook, covered, over high heat for 3 minutes. Drain the spinach and chop finely with a knife.

❦ Heat 1 tablespoon oil in a nonstick 10-in (26-cm) skillet. Add onion and cook, stirring, over low heat for 3 minutes or until golden, then add garlic and cook for 1 minute more.

❦ Beat the egg in a bowl, add the cheese and mash with a fork. Add the spinach, parsley, the contents of the skillet and half the breadcrumbs. Season with salt, pepper and nutmeg and stir well.

❦ Preheat an oven to 450°F (230°C). Using some of the remaining oil, lightly oil a baking dish large enough to hold half the sardines in a single layer. Arrange half the sardines in the dish and spread each one with a spoonful of the stuffing mixture. Cover each sardine with a second one and pour the rest of the oil over. Sprinkle with breadcrumbs and bake for 20 minutes. Serve hot, warm or cold, directly from the baking dish.

Serves 6

GRAND AÏOLI

AÏOLI FEAST

The word aïoli *is Provençal, derived from* ail *(garlic) and* huile *(oil). The sauce gives its name to this dish, which in Provence is often served on Good Friday.*

4 lb (2 kg) salt cod fillets
2 lb (1 kg) shellfish (large sea snails, whelks, clams or cockles)
salt and freshly ground pepper
10 small artichokes
2 lb (1 kg) small carrots, peeled
2 lb (1 kg) small leeks, trimmed
1 lb (500 g) small green beans
10 boiling potatoes, peeled
1 cauliflower, separated into small florets
10 eggs

FOR THE *AÏOLI*:
6 cloves garlic
2 teaspoons strong mustard
3 egg yolks
salt
2 cups (16 fl oz/500 ml) extra virgin olive oil

✢ Soak cod in a bowl of cold water, skin side up, for 12 hours, changing the water 3 times.
✢ Rinse the shellfish and place in a saucepan. Cover with cold water and bring to boil. Remove the scum during the first 5 minutes of cooking, then season liberally with salt and simmer gently for 45 minutes. Drain the shellfish and either leave them in their shells or remove them and keep warm.
✢ Discard the bruised outside leaves of the artichokes and trim the heart, cutting off the spiky tips. Cook all the vegetables separately in boiling salted water until slightly crisp. Drain and keep warm. Hard-cook the eggs for 10 minutes, then cool and shell.
✢ Drain the cod and transfer to a large pot of cold water, skin side down. Bring to boil over low heat, then reduce heat and cook at the barest simmer for 10 minutes. Drain and cool.

❧ Meanwhile, prepare the *aïoli:* force the garlic through a press into a shallow bowl. Add the mustard, egg yolks and salt and stir well. Set aside for 1 minute, then add the oil in a thin stream, whisking until the mixture is quite firm. (The *aïoli* may also be made in a food processor.)

❧ Arrange the lukewarm salt cod, shellfish and vegetables on a large platter. Add the hard-cooked eggs, and offer the *aïoli* separately: each diner takes a little *aïoli* and dips the pieces of salt cod, shellfish and vegetables into it before eating them.

Serves 8–10

ESCABÈCHE OF RED MULLET

6 tablespoons (3 fl oz/90 ml) extra virgin
    olive oil
6 tablespoons (3 fl oz/90 ml) red wine
    vinegar
3 oz (100 g) fresh mint leaves

❧ Ask the fishmonger to scale and gut the
fish, leaving the livers intact. Rinse the fish
and pat dry; season with salt and pepper.

❧ Heat the oil in a nonstick 10-in (26-cm)
skillet and cook the fish for 4 minutes on each
side. Drain on paper towels and lay in a
shallow dish. Transfer 4 tablespoons of the
cooking oil to a small saucepan.

❧ Pour the vinegar into a second small nonaluminum saucepan and add the mint leaves.
Bring to boil, stir and remove from heat.
Pour this mixture into the reserved oil and
boil for a few seconds, then pour over the fish.
Allow the fish to cool. Let stand for at least
4 hours before serving.

Serves 4

Provence

ROUGETS EN ESCABÈCHE
ESCABÈCHE OF RED MULLET

*Escabèche is a vinegar marinade of Spanish origin
created for preserving little fried fish from which the
heads have been removed: hence the name, which
comes from* cabeza, *the Spanish word for head.
Today, whole fish such as redfish, mackerel and
whiting, and cutlets of tuna, bonito, swordfish or
hake are also prepared in this manner.*

8 red mullet, about 6 oz (200 g) each
salt and freshly ground pepper

Provence

BOURRIDE
BOURRIDE

The link between the bourride de lotte *of Languedoc
and the Provençal* bourride *is aïoli. But whereas
the first is made only with anglerfish and includes
a very thick sauce, the second is a true thick soup,
containing every variety of white-fleshed fish.*

4 lb (2 kg) mixed white fish: monkfish
    (anglerfish) or blue-eye cod, sea bass,
    John Dory, turbot or flounder . . .
1 carrot, peeled and coarsely chopped

1 onion, coarsely chopped

2 leeks, white parts only, well washed and
   coarsely chopped

6 cloves garlic

bouquet garni: 1 bay leaf, 1 sprig thyme,
   1 sprig dried fennel, 6 sprigs parsley,
   1 strip dried orange peel (tied together)

2 cups (16 fl oz/500 ml) dry white wine

3 cups (24 fl oz/750 ml) water

salt and freshly ground pepper

FOR THE SAUCE:

3 cloves garlic

1 teaspoon strong mustard

2 egg yolks

salt

1 cup (8 fl oz/250 ml) extra virgin olive oil

FOR SERVING:

slices of toasted baguette (French bread)

cloves of garlic, halved

❧ Ask the fishmonger to scale and gut the
fish and remove the heads, reserving the
heads and bones. Cut the fish into 1½-in
(4-cm) chunks.

❧ Place the fish heads and bones in a large
saucepan. Add the carrot, onion, leeks, garlic,
bouquet garni, wine and water and bring to
simmer. Season with salt and pepper and
simmer for 20 minutes.

❧ Meanwhile, prepare the sauce: force the
garlic through a press into a shallow bowl.
Add the mustard, egg yolk and salt and stir
well. Set aside for 1 minute, then add the oil
in a thin stream, whisking until the mixture
is quite firm; this *aïoli* will thicken the sauce.

❧ Strain the stock into another saucepan.
Bring the stock to simmer over low heat and

add the fish. Simmer, covered, for 10 minutes.

❧ Remove the cooked fish from the stock
with a slotted spoon and keep warm in a
tureen. Blend half the *aïoli* into the stock, off
the heat. Pour this sauce over the fish and
serve immediately, accompanied by toasted
bread rubbed with garlic and spread with the
remaining *aïoli*.

Serves 6   *Photograph page 36*

Pays Basque

ANCHOIS AU TXAKOLI
ANCHOVIES IN TXAKOLI WINE

2 lb (1 kg) fresh anchovies

5 tablespoons (2½ oz/75 g) butter

1 lb (500 g) onions, finely chopped

4 cloves garlic, finely chopped

1 fresh chili pepper, seeded and minced

6 tablespoons (3 fl oz/90 ml) *txakoli*
   (dry white) wine

salt and freshly ground pepper

❧ Remove the heads from the anchovies and
gut them. Rinse and pat dry with paper
towels. Melt the butter in a nonstick 10-in
(26-cm) sauté pan. Add the onion, garlic and
pepper and cook, stirring, for 2 minutes. Add
the anchovies and wine and cook for about
10 minutes over high heat, turning the
anchovies so that they cook on both sides.
Season with salt and pepper. Remove from
heat, cover and let the anchovies rest for
10 minutes before serving.

Serves 4   *Photograph pages 42–43*

ROUGETS À LA NIÇOISE
RED MULLET NICE STYLE

Redfish liver is particularly tasty, so take care not to discard it when you are gutting the fish. It can be left to cook in the fish or puréed raw and mixed into anchovy butter, which is used as a sauce for grilled fish.

8 red mullet, about 6 oz (180 g) each
salt and freshly ground pepper
1 lb (500 g) ripe tomatoes
¼ cup (2 fl oz/60 ml) extra virgin
   olive oil
1 onion, finely chopped
3 cloves garlic, finely chopped
8 anchovy fillets in oil
2 oz (50 g) small black Niçoise olives

❧ Ask the fishmonger to scale and gut the fish, leaving the livers intact. Rinse the fish and pat dry; season with salt and pepper. Drop the tomatoes into boiling water for 10 seconds. Cool under running water, peel, halve and squeeze out the seeds.

❧ Heat half the oil in a nonstick 10-in (26-cm) sauté pan and cook the chopped onion and garlic until soft and golden. Stir in the tomatoes, season with salt and pepper and cook over high heat for 5 minutes.

❧ Heat the rest of the oil in a nonstick 10-in (26-cm) skillet and cook the fish for 4 minutes each side. Drain and arrange on a heated serving platter. Cover with the tomato sauce and garnish with anchovy fillets and olives. Serve immediately.

Serves 4

DAURADE À LA PROVENÇALE
BAKED BREAM PROVENÇAL STYLE

1 bream or carp, about 2½ lb (1.2 kg)
1 lb (500 g) ripe tomatoes
¼ cup (2 fl oz/60 ml) extra virgin olive oil
2 cloves garlic, finely chopped
1 tablespoon chopped flat-leaf parsley
salt and freshly ground pepper
1 lemon

❧ Ask the fishmonger to scale and gut the fish; rinse it and pat dry.

❧ Preheat an oven to 450°F (230°C). Drop the tomatoes into boiling water for 10 seconds. Cool under running water, then peel, halve, squeeze out seeds and coarsely chop the flesh.

❧ Heat half the oil in a nonstick 10-in (26-cm) skillet. Add the garlic and parsley and cook, stirring, until the garlic is soft and golden. Stir in the tomatoes and season with salt and pepper. Cook over moderate heat until the liquid from the tomatoes has almost entirely evaporated, about 5 minutes.

❧ Lay the fish in a baking dish just large enough to hold it. Sprinkle with the remaining oil and turn so that all the surfaces are coated with oil. Bake for 5 minutes.

❧ Meanwhile, wash and dry the lemon and cut into thin rounds. Cover the fish with the tomato sauce. Arrange the lemon slices over the fish and bake for 30 minutes longer. Serve directly from the dish.

Serves 4

PHOTOGRAPHED IN PROVENCE: GRILLED SEA BASS
WITH FENNEL (TOP LEFT, RECIPE PAGE 44),
RED MULLET NICE STYLE (BOTTOM LEFT) AND
BAKED BREAM PROVENÇAL STYLE (BOTTOM RIGHT)

POULTRY AND GAME

I T ALL BEGAN with the Sunday *poule au pot,* which Henri IV, much-beloved king of France, wished to provide as festive fare for all his subjects. Over five centuries, many changes have taken place: chicken has become an economical, even everyday dish.

The finest of all, the greatest luxury, is the Bresse chicken: white-feathered, blue-clawed, allowed 10 square meters' space each, fed on grain. The poultry is superb, with tender, juicy and tasty flesh, the gentle and soothing reflection of a fertile earth. In Bresse, chickens are treated like children.

Poultry appeals to all palates, lends itself to all kinds of preparations and all vegetables, adapts to all traditions. With cream, with tarragon, with vinegar, with wild mushrooms from the forest, with rich *vin jaune,* with freshwater crayfish, with garlic, with cider, with butter, with mustard, stuffed, poached in stock, cooked with rice, with a cream sauce known as *suprême,* with peppers, with truffles, with beer, with champagne, with Riesling: every region has its own recipe.

The *coq,* or rooster (typically a bird at least one year of age, its reproductive duties already past), is traditionally cooked *au vin,* either red, white or *jaune,* in order to tenderize its somewhat tough flesh.

As for the duck, it is the foundation of some of the great French dishes. Its special quality is a firm, substantial flesh, which can be cooked rare like steak and which lends itself to sweet-sour combinations, to the flavor of the orange, to sauces enriched with liver, or *foie gras* or the juices extracted from the carcass by means of a silver duck press.

More and more often, the fillets of the fattened duck, called *magrets* or *maigrets,* are cooked rare, following a fashion initiated in Gers by the chef of Auch, André Daguin. In effect, they are duck "steaks."

The rabbit, for many years disregarded and relegated to everyday fare, has made a triumphant return to the table. But regional traditions never abandoned the rabbit, accompanying it with prunes, mustard or cider and inviting gourmets to partake of its plump thighs and also its saddle (the meaty part from the end of the ribs to the tail). As a *civet* or *à la royale,* stuffed with *foie gras* and served with a sauce flavored with its organ meats, with pan-fried fruits such as quinces and pears, with a chestnut purée or with fresh pasta, it is the tastiest of autumn fare.

RABBIT PARCELS (LEFT, RECIPE PAGE 56) AND CHICKEN WITH FORTY CLOVES OF GARLIC (RIGHT, RECIPE PAGE 55), PHOTOGRAPHED IN PROVENCE

CHICKEN CASSEROLE

Auvergne / Bourgogne

COQ AU VIN

CHICKEN CASSEROLE

This dish was originally made with Chanturgues, a red wine from Auvergne. This has become rare and is now replaced by red wine from Bourgogne. However, every province in France claims to have invented the dish, and indeed similar preparations based on red or white wine are found almost everywhere.

1 chicken, about 4 lb (2 kg), cut into 10
    serving pieces
salt and freshly ground pepper
⅓ cup (2 oz/60 g) all-purpose (plain) flour
1 slice streaky bacon, about 3 oz (100 g)
24 small (button) mushrooms
1 tablespoon vegetable oil
3 tablespoons butter
24 small pickling onions, peeled
2 tablespoons cognac
3 cups (24 fl oz/750 ml) red Burgundy, such
    as Chambertin
3 cloves garlic
bouquet garni: 1 bay leaf, 1 sprig thyme,
    1 sprig rosemary, 8 sprigs parsley
    (tied together)
4 pinches freshly grated nutmeg

1 teaspoon sugar
croutons

❧ Season the chicken with salt and pepper. Spread the flour on a plate and roll the chicken pieces in it, shaking off excess.

❧ Cut the bacon into fine matchsticks, removing the rind. Trim the mushrooms, wash and pat dry.

❧ Heat the oil in a 6-qt (6-l) pot and add the butter. Cook the onions, bacon and mushrooms until softened, then remove and set aside. Brown the chicken pieces on all sides for about 10 minutes. Sprinkle in the cognac and ignite, shaking the pot gently until flames subside. Pour in the wine and stir in the bouquet garni, garlic, salt, pepper, nutmeg and sugar. Bring to simmer and cook the chicken for 1 hour, stirring from time to time. Add the mushroom mixture and cook for 30 minutes longer.

❧ Remove the cooked chicken pieces from the pot and arrange on a serving platter. Remove the bouquet garni and let the sauce boil over high heat for 2 minutes or until thickened. Pour over the chicken and serve immediately, accompanied by croutons.

Serves 6

Provence

POULET AUX QUARANTE GOUSSES D'AIL

CHICKEN WITH FORTY CLOVES OF GARLIC

In Provence, where it is called the poor man's truffle, garlic is the basis of the local cuisine. Braised en chemise ("in a shirt"—in other words, *unpeeled), the garlic cloves become soft and creamy, making a delicious purée that enhances the flavor of poultry.*

1 chicken, about 3½ lb (1.75 kg)
salt
2 sprigs fresh thyme
2 sprigs fresh rosemary
2 sprigs fresh sage
2 tender celery stalks, with their leaves
2 sprigs flat-leaf parsley
40 cloves fresh, young garlic, unpeeled
3 tablespoons olive oil
freshly ground pepper
toasted slices of country bread

❧ Preheat an oven to 400°F (200°C). Sprinkle the chicken with salt inside and out. Stuff the chicken with half the thyme, rosemary, sage and celery; add the parsley and 4 cloves of garlic. Place the remaining herbs and celery in an oval earthenware or enameled pot just large enough to hold the chicken. Add the oil, salt, pepper and remaining garlic cloves. Roll the chicken in the oil to coat on all sides. Cover the pot and bake for 1¾ hours.

❧ Transfer the cooked chicken to a serving platter and surround it with the cloves of garlic. Skim the fat from the cooking juices and pour into a sauceboat. Serve the chicken hot, accompanied by its sauce and toasted slices of bread. Each diner crushes the garlic slightly to remove the skin and spreads the wonderful fragrant purée that is left onto a slice of bread.

Serves 5–6   *Photograph page 52*

Provence

LAPIN EN PAQUETS
RABBIT PARCELS

It is the method of preparation that gives this dish its name: each piece of rabbit is enclosed in a "packet" of bacon. Rabbit is cooked this way throughout Provence, and sometimes fried eggplant (aubergine) slices are used instead of the tomatoes.

8 oz (250 g) ripe tomatoes
2 tablespoons olive oil
salt and freshly ground pepper
2 pinches sugar
1 rabbit, about 3¼ lb (1.6 kg), cut into
   8 serving pieces
8 very thin slices streaky bacon
8 small sprigs thyme
2 cloves garlic, finely slivered

❧ Preheat an oven to 400°F (200°C). Drop the tomatoes into boiling water for 10 seconds. Cool under running water, then peel, halve, squeeze out the seeds and coarsely chop the flesh. Combine the tomatoes and 1 tablespoon olive oil in a nonstick 10-in (26-cm) sauté pan. Add salt, pepper and sugar and cook over high heat, stirring constantly, until reduced to a thick purée.

❧ Using the remaining oil, grease a shallow baking dish large enough to hold the rabbit pieces in one layer. Pour in the tomato purée.

❧ Rinse the rabbit and pat dry; season with salt and pepper. Place a piece of rabbit in the center of a slice of bacon. Season with a sprig of thyme and a few slivers of garlic. Wrap the bacon around the rabbit and secure with a toothpick. Repeat with the remaining ingredients.

❧ Arrange the rabbit "parcels" on the tomato purée and bake for 1 hour, turning the parcels after 30 minutes.

❧ Remove the toothpicks and arrange the rabbit parcels on a serving platter. Cover with the tomato sauce and serve immediately.

Serves 4   *Photograph page 52*

Languedoc

FOIE GRAS FRAIS AUX RAISINS
FRESH FOIE GRAS WITH GRAPES

This version of the classic dish in the grand tradition of French cuisine has been simplified so that only the true taste of the fresh foie gras comes through.

1 cup (5 oz/150 g) white muscat grapes
4 slices fresh duck *foie gras,* about 3 oz
   (80 g) each and ½ in (1 cm) thick, chilled
salt and freshly ground pepper
1 tablespoon Armagnac

❧ Peel the grapes and remove the seeds, working over a plate to catch the juice.

❧ Heat a nonstick skillet over moderate heat. Season the slices of *foie gras* with salt and pepper. Cook them for 40 seconds on each side or until a crusty surface forms. Arrange them on 2 heated plates.

❧ Discard the fat in the pan and pour in the Armagnac and grape juice. Boil the liquid until reduced by half. Add the grapes to the pan and mix for 30 seconds. Surround the slices of *foie gras* with grapes, pour the sauce over and serve immediately.

Serves 2   *Photograph page 61*

DUCK WITH CHERRIES

CANARD MONTMORENCY

DUCK WITH CHERRIES

Montmorency is the name of a variety of small cherry—a bittersweet morello that is excellent for cooking. It is used in a number of dishes, both savory and sweet.

1 duck, about 3 lb (1.5 kg)
salt and freshly ground pepper
1 lb (500 g) Montmorency cherries
⅔ cup (5 fl oz/150 ml) dry white wine
1 teaspoon sugar
1 teaspoon arrowroot
3 tablespoons cherry brandy

❧ Preheat an oven to 425°F (215°C). Season the duck inside and out with salt and pepper. Place in roasting pan and roast for 1 hour, basting frequently with the cooking juices.

Meanwhile, pit the cherries, catching all juices.
❧ Remove the cooked duck from the oven, tilting it so that any juices inside the bird will run into the pan. Transfer to a plate and keep warm. Skim the fat from the juices in the roasting pan. Place the pan over high heat, pour in the wine and deglaze the pan, scraping up browned bits with a wooden spoon. Boil until reduced by half. Transfer to a small saucepan and add the cherry juice and sugar.
❧ Bring the contents of the saucepan to boil. Blend together the arrowroot and brandy and pour into the boiling sauce. Boil, stirring constantly, until the sauce thickens, about 2 minutes. Add cherries and remove from heat.
❧ Carve the duck and arrange on a serving plate. Surround it with a few cherries. Pour the remaining sauce and cherries into a sauceboat and serve immediately.

Serves 4

Savoie

POULET AU COMTÉ

CHICKEN WITH COMTÉ CHEESE

This delicious dish is equally good whether it is made in Savoie, in Franche-Comté or in the Lyonnais region, where it is simply called poulet au fromage. *Sometimes half the* comté *cheese is replaced by Emmenthaler.*

1 chicken, about 3¼ lb (1.6 kg), cut into
    8 serving pieces
salt and freshly ground pepper
1 tablespoon vegetable oil
¾ cup (6 fl oz/200 ml) dry white wine,
    preferably from Savoie
2 tablespoons strong mustard
3 oz (100 g) *comté* cheese, freshly and finely
    grated

✛ Preheat an oven to 425°F (215°C). Season the chicken with salt and pepper. Heat the oil in a nonstick 10-in (26-cm) sauté pan and lightly brown the chicken pieces on all sides. Remove the chicken from the pan and discard the oil. Pour in the wine and deglaze the pan, using a wooden spoon to scrape up the browned bits. Blend the mustard into the wine.
✛ Arrange the chicken pieces in a baking dish large enough to hold them in a single layer. Pour over the sauce from the pan. Bake for 40 minutes, turning the chicken from time to time.
✛ Sprinkle the chicken with grated cheese and cook for 5 minutes longer or until the cheese melts and starts to brown. Serve hot, directly from the dish.

Serves 6

Bourgogne

POULE AU RIZ

CHICKEN WITH RICE

This simple, invigorating family dish is prepared in every French home. Sometimes the rice is sprinkled with finely grated Emmenthaler.

1 chicken, about 4 lb (2 kg), with liver,
    gizzard, heart and neck
salt and freshly ground pepper
8 oz (250 g) carrots
1 tablespoon vegetable oil
2 tablespoons butter
3 onions, finely chopped
2 cups (16 fl oz/500 ml) white Burgundy
1¼ cups (10 fl oz/300 ml) water
bouquet garni: 1 bay leaf, 1 sprig thyme,
    6 sprigs parsley (tied together)
1⅔ cups (11 oz/350 g) long-grain rice

✛ Season the chicken inside and out with salt and pepper. Peel the carrots and quarter them lengthwise, then cut into ¼-in (.5-cm) fan-shaped slices.
✛ Heat the oil in a 4-qt (4-l) pot and lightly brown the chicken on all sides. Remove from the pot and discard the oil. Place the butter, carrots and onions in the pot and soften over low heat, stirring constantly with a wooden spoon. Add the chicken liver, gizzard, heart and neck and cook for a further minute. Return the chicken to the pot, add the wine and water and bring to simmer. Add the bouquet garni, salt and pepper. Turn the chicken onto its side, cover the pot and cook over very gentle heat for 1 hour.
✛ Turn the chicken over to its other side and simmer gently for another hour.

CHICKEN WITH RICE (TOP), BASQUE CHICKEN (BOTTOM LEFT, RECIPE PAGE 60) AND CHICKEN WITH COMTÉ CHEESE (BOTTOM RIGHT)

❧ Place the chicken on its back and sprinkle the rice around it. Cover and cook for 30 minutes longer over low heat, without stirring.

❧ Remove the chicken and place it on a serving platter. Discard the chicken innards and neck and the bouquet garni; stir the rice with a fork. Surround the chicken with the rice and serve.

Serves 6

Pays Basque

POULET BASQUAISE
BASQUE CHICKEN

4 small green peppers (capsicums)
1 lb (500 g) ripe tomatoes
1 chicken, about 3 lb (1.5 kg), cut into
    8 serving pieces
salt and freshly ground pepper
3 tablespoons vegetable oil
2 onions, finely chopped
3 cloves garlic, finely chopped
1 slice prosciutto or Bayonne ham, about
    5 oz (150 g), cut into small cubes
1 fresh chili pepper, seeded and finely
    chopped
⅔ cup (5 fl oz/150 ml) dry white wine

❧ Cut the green peppers in half and remove the stems, seeds and white ribs. Cut the flesh into fine strips. Drop the tomatoes into boiling water for 10 seconds. Cool under running water, peel, halve and squeeze out the seeds; finely chop the flesh.
❧ Season the chicken with salt and pepper. Heat the oil in a nonstick 10-in (26-cm) sauté pan and lightly brown the chicken pieces on all sides. Remove from the pan. Add the onions and garlic and stir for 1 minute. Add the ham, peppers and chili and cook over low heat, stirring, for 5 minutes or until the vegetables soften and are lightly browned.
❧ Return the chicken pieces to the pan, pour in the wine and let it evaporate over high heat. Add the tomatoes and season with salt and pepper. Cover and cook the chicken over low heat for 45 minutes, stirring from time to time.

❧ Transfer the chicken to a shallow dish. Boil the cooking liquid over high heat until thick. Pour over the chicken and serve immediately.

Serves 4–6   *Photograph page 59*

Languedoc

MAGRETS GRILLÉS SAUCE AILLADE
BREAST OF DUCK WITH GARLIC SAUCE

Sauce aillade, *which is particularly appreciated in Toulouse, may be made using equal amounts of olive oil and walnut oil. Breast of duck served with this fragrant sauce is excellent accompanied with sautéed* cèpes.

2 cloves garlic, coarsely chopped
3 tablespoons Armagnac
1 sprig thyme, crumbled
salt and freshly ground pepper
2 fresh duck breasts, 12 oz (350 g) each
24 fresh walnuts, shelled and peeled
3 cloves garlic, halved
2 tablespoons water
6 tablespoons (3 fl oz/90 ml) extra virgin
    olive oil

❧ Combine the chopped garlic, Armagnac and thyme in a bowl and season with salt and pepper. Add the duck breasts and turn to coat. Let marinate at room temperature for 1 hour, turning often.
❧ Combine the walnuts, halved garlic cloves and water in a food processor and blend to a thick paste. Season with salt and pepper. With the machine running, pour in the oil

in a thin stream to produce an emulsified sauce. Transfer to a sauceboat and set aside.

✤ Drain the duck breasts, reserving marinade. Pat them dry and wipe off the garlic. Heat an enameled 4-qt (4-l) pot over moderate heat and lay the duck breasts on the bottom, skin side down. Cook for 8 minutes, basting the meat with the fat given out during cooking. Discard the fat, turn the breasts over and cook for 5 minutes longer, pricking the skin with a fork to allow some of the fat to escape. Remove the duck from the pot and discard all fat. Strain the reserved marinade into the pot and boil for 1 minute, then remove from heat. Return the duck breasts to the pot, skin-side down, cover and let rest for 15 minutes.

✤ Remove the duck from the pot and slice thinly. Divide slices among four heated plates. Add to the pot any juices that have escaped during slicing. Pour this sauce over the duck and serve immediately, accompanied by the garlic sauce.

Serves 4

BREAST OF DUCK WITH GARLIC SAUCE (TOP) AND FRESH FOIS GRAS WITH GRAPES (BOTTOM, RECIPE PAGE 56)

DUCK WITH ORANGE

Orléanais

CANARD À L'ORANGE

DUCK WITH ORANGE

1 duck, about 3 lb (1.5 kg)
salt and freshly ground pepper
1 tablespoon vegetable oil
6 oranges
1 lemon
¼ cup (2½ oz/75 g) sugar
2 tablespoons water
3 tablespoons red wine vinegar
6 tablespoons (3 fl oz/90 ml) dry white wine
1 teaspoon arrowroot

3 tablespoons curaçao
1 tablespoon red currant jelly

❧ Preheat an oven to 425°F (215°C). Season duck inside and out with salt and pepper. Place the duck in a greased roasting pan and roast for 1 hour, basting regularly with the pan juices.
❧ Meanwhile, wash and dry the oranges and lemon. Carefully remove zest from the lemon and two of the oranges with a zester. Squeeze the juice of these three fruits into a bowl. Peel the remaining oranges so that no trace of white pith is left, collecting any juice in the bowl. Separate the oranges into segments.

❧ Heat the sugar and water in a saucepan over low heat until the sugar caramelizes to a light golden color. Add the vinegar and citrus juices and boil for 1 minute. Set aside.

❧ Remove the cooked duck from the oven, tilting it so that any juices inside the bird will run into the pan. Keep warm on a plate.

❧ Skim the fat from the roasting juices. Add the wine and deglaze the pan over high heat, scraping up browned bits with a wooden spoon. Boil until the liquid is reduced by half. Transfer to a small saucepan and return to boil. Add the citrus mixture. Blend the arrowroot and curaçao in a small bowl, then pour into the boiling sauce with the red currant jelly. Boil, stirring constantly, until the sauce thickens, about 2 minutes. Stir in the zest and the orange segments and remove from heat.

❧ Carve the duck and arrange it on a serving plate. Remove some of the orange segments from the sauce with a slotted spoon and arrange around the duck. Pour the sauce into a sauceboat and serve immediately.

Serves 4

Bretagne / Normandie

LAPIN AU CIDRE
RABBIT IN CIDER

1 rabbit, about 3¼ lb (1.6 kg), cut into
   9 pieces (reserve liver)
salt and freshly ground pepper
1 slice streaky bacon, about 3 oz (100 g)
3 oz (100 g) small fresh *cèpes* (*porcini* mushrooms)
1 tablespoon vegetable oil
2 tablespoons butter
4 French shallots, finely chopped
2 tablespoons *calvados*
1 cup (8 fl oz/250 ml) dry cider
1 egg yolk
1 tablespoon strong mustard
6 tablespoons (3 fl oz/90 ml) heavy (double)
   cream or crème fraîche

❧ Rinse the rabbit and pat dry; season with salt and pepper. Cut the bacon into small strips, removing the rind. Trim, wash, dry and quarter the mushrooms.

❧ Heat the oil in a nonstick 11-in (28-cm) sauté pan. Add the butter and gently cook the shallots, bacon and mushrooms, stirring constantly with a wooden spoon. Scrape this mixture from the pan, add the rabbit pieces and brown on all sides for 10 minutes. Pour in the *calvados* and let it evaporate. Stir in the cider and bring to boil, then cover and cook over low heat for 30 minutes, turning two or three times. After 30 minutes, return the bacon, mushrooms and shallots to the pan and simmer for 15 minutes longer.

❧ In a bowl beat the egg yolk, mustard and cream. Add the uncooked rabbit liver, pushing it through a sieve, and mix well.

❧ Remove the cooked rabbit from the sauté pan with a slotted spoon and arrange in a serving dish with the mushrooms and bacon. Boil the cooking liquid over high heat until reduced to a syrupy consistency. Pour the mustard mixture into the pan and stir for 30 seconds, then remove from heat. Whisk the sauce until smooth and creamy. Pour it over the rabbit and serve immediately.

Serves 4   *Photograph page 65*

Normandie

POULET VALLÉE D'AUGE
CHICKEN WITH MUSHROOM SAUCE

This recipe takes its name from the Vallée d'Auge in Normandie, which is renowned for its apples. It includes butter, cream and calvados, *all basic ingredients of the cuisine of Normandie.*

1 chicken, about 3 lb (1.5 kg), cut into
   8 serving pieces
salt and freshly ground pepper
1 tart apple
1 tablespoon vegetable oil
3 tablespoons butter
2 tablespoons *calvados*
1 tablespoon water
1 lb (500 g) mushrooms
⅔ cup (5 fl oz/150 ml) heavy (double) cream
   or crème fraîche

✤ Season the chicken with salt and pepper. Peel and core the apple and cut into ½-in (1-cm) cubes.
✤ Heat the oil in a nonstick 10-in (26-cm) sauté pan. Add half the butter and, as soon as it has melted, lightly brown the chicken pieces on all sides, turning them with a wooden spoon. Add the apple and mix for 1 minute. Pour in the *calvados* and ignite, shaking the pan gently until flames subside. Stir in the water, cover and cook over very low heat for 45 minutes.
✤ Meanwhile, trim the mushrooms, rinse and pat dry. Slice thinly. Melt the remaining butter in a nonstick 10-in (26-cm) skillet and cook the mushrooms over high heat until they are golden and give out no more liquid.

✤ Remove the cooked chicken pieces from the pan and keep warm on a platter. Boil the cooking liquid until reduced to a syrupy consistency. Add the cream and boil over high heat for about 2 minutes, stirring with a wooden spoon, until the sauce is thick and smooth. Add the mushrooms and stir for 1 minute. Pour the sauce over the chicken pieces and serve immediately.

Serves 4–6

Normandie

POULET À LA CRÈME À L'ESTRAGON
CHICKEN WITH CREAM AND TARRAGON

1 chicken, about 3½ lb (1.75 kg)
salt
10 sprigs fresh tarragon
2 tablespoons butter
¾ cup (6 fl oz/200 ml) chicken stock
   (recipe page 120)
¾ cup (6 fl oz/200 ml) heavy (double) cream
   or crème fraîche

✤ Season the chicken inside and out with salt. Place 8 sprigs of tarragon inside the cavity of the chicken.
✤ Melt the butter in a pot just large enough to hold the chicken. Brown the chicken on all sides for about 10 minutes. Remove from the pot and discard the butter. Pour in the stock and deglaze the pot, scraping up browned bits with a wooden spoon. Return the chicken to the pot, cover and cook over low heat for 1 hour and 20 minutes.
✤ Meanwhile, strip the leaves from the reserved tarragon and chop finely. Remove

RABBIT IN CIDER (TOP LEFT, RECIPE PAGE 63), CHICKEN WITH MUSHROOM SAUCE (TOP RIGHT) AND
CHICKEN WITH CREAM AND TARRAGON (BOTTOM), PHOTOGRAPHED IN NORMANDIE

the cooked chicken from the pot and keep warm. Boil the cooking juices until reduced to a syrupy consistency, then add the cream and boil for 2 minutes longer. Stir in the chopped tarragon and remove from heat.

Carve the chicken into portions and arrange on a serving plate. Pour the cream sauce over and serve immediately.

Serves 4–6

MEATS

ALTHOUGH THEY MAY CLAIM to have a passion for fish, reputedly lighter, more healthy and more sympathetic to the chef's culinary fantasies, the French adore meat.

The French herd of beef cattle numbers about 25 million, spread among various breeds: Limousin, Salers, Aubrac, Maine Anjou, Blonde Aquitaine, and above all the Charolais, which are the most acclaimed.

Braised, boiled or pan-fried, beef is robust and handsome. The *entrecôte*, tender and with a nice cover of fat, is a cut worthy of a king, much appreciated when pan-fried and served with a sauce based on shallots and red wine (known as Bercy or *marchand de vin* sauce). Red wine and beef also combine in Burgundian-style beef, in the *daube* or with beef cooked as a *civet*. Or the beef might be cooked in a consommé, lowered into the liquid and taken out by means of a string (*ficelle*)—hence the name *boeuf à la ficelle*.

Veal comes from a young, unweaned calf—that is, one that has been nourished solely on milk, natural or reconstituted, then slaughtered at between one and four months.

Racks of veal cut between the ninth and thirteenth rib make the tender, juicy cutlets that, like their sister the *escalope* (often replaced by more economical turkey in everyday French cuisine), are gently pan-fried, simmered in their juices with cream and mushrooms, or

breaded. The family-style *blanquette de veau*, is customarily accompanied by rice. It is the perfect example of a bourgeois dish.

Aged from one to six months, lamb provides meat that is more tender and delicate than that of older sheep. The most highly ranked is from Sisteron, in Upper Provence; its flavor reflects the animal's diet of wild thyme, rosemary, savory and sage. Thus a "simple" Provençal roast of lamb, which might be studded with garlic, scents the air with the perfume of the land where it lived.

Pré salé lamb, which has grazed on the salty pastures around the peninsula of Mont-Saint-Michel, is also highly regarded. The leg, or *gigot* is a favorite among the French, often served on Sundays accompanied by flageolet beans. Every cut of lamb is flavorful: chops, rack, neck, saddle, shoulder and breast, which may be simply grilled. Whether a slow-simmered dish in a *daube* or *navarin*, or simply spit-roasted, lamb remains a royal dish, one of the few things about which the French always seem to agree.

Prized by the people of eastern France, pork goes well with beer and cabbage, is the starting point for charcuterie (ham, *terrines, pâtés)*, and indeed is the natural accompaniment of the traditional sauerkraut. In Alsace, in the north, in Lorraine, the marriage of the gourmet and the pig has always been celebrated in traditional dishes.

VEAL IN WHITE SAUCE (LEFT, RECIPE PAGE 70), POACHED BEEF ON A STRING (TOP RIGHT, RECIPE PAGE 68) AND LAMB WITH SPRING VEGETABLES (BOTTOM RIGHT, RECIPE PAGE 78), PHOTOGRAPHED IN ILE-DE-FRANCE

Île-de-France

BOEUF À LA FICELLE
POACHED BEEF ON A STRING

The name of this dish undoubtedly comes from the phrase pelican à la ficelle. *The pelican is an atrophied muscle on the heart side of the animal, which the butchers kept for themselves. When their work was finished they would go to a restaurant in the Villette quarter of Paris and cook this piece of meat in a large pot of boiling salted water. In order to recognize his piece, each butcher would attach it to a length of string carrying his number. This* pelican *was eaten with coarse salt as soon as it was cooked.*

4 pieces of beef rump, fillet or tenderloin, each about 5 oz (150 g) and 1¼ in (3 cm) thick
salt and freshly ground pepper
3 qt (3 l) beef stock

FOR SERVING:
coarse salt
a variety of mustards
cornichons (small French sour pickles or gherkins)

✤ Tie the pieces of beef with string as you would a parcel, leaving a loop 2½ in (6 cm) long at the center. Season the beef with salt and pepper.
✤ Pour the stock into a 4-qt (4-l) pot and bring to boil. Slip the handle of a wooden spoon under the string loops so that the pieces of meat are suspended from it. Rest the spoon on the sides of the pot. Poach 4 minutes for steaks that will be pink at the center, or more or less to taste. Remove the meat from the stock and place one piece on each of 4 warmed plates. Serve immediately, accompanied by coarse salt, mustards and cornichons.

Serves 4   *Photograph page 66*

Bourgogne

BOEUF BOURGUIGNON
BURGUNDY BEEF

8 oz (250 g) pork belly
1 tablespoon vegetable oil
3 tablespoons butter
36 small pickling onions, peeled
3 lb 10 oz (1.8 kg) beef suitable for braising, such as round, topside or chuck steak
3 tablespoons *marc de Bourgogne* or brandy
3 cups (24 fl oz/750 ml) red Burgundy
36 small (button) mushrooms
1 tablespoon fresh lemon juice
salt and freshly ground pepper
2 teaspoons arrowroot
2 tablespoons cold water

✤ Rinse the pork belly under running water, then cut into thin strips. Drop into boiling water, blanch for 5 minutes; drain and rinse.
✤ Heat the oil in a 6-qt (6-l) pot and cook the strips of pork belly over low heat until golden brown, about 5 minutes, stirring constantly. Remove from the pot with a slotted spoon and set aside.
✤ Add a little less than half the butter to the pot and cook the onions over very low heat until golden, turning frequently, about 10 minutes. Remove with a slotted spoon and add to the pork.

❧ Cut the meat into 2-in (5-cm) cubes. Cook in the pot in batches until lightly browned, about 5 minutes, turning frequently. Set aside.

❧ Discard the fat from the pot. Add the *marc* and, 1 minute later, the wine, scraping up browned bits with a wooden spoon. Ignite the wine and wait until flames subside. Return the meat to the pot and bring to simmer. Cover and cook over very low heat for 3 hours.

❧ Meanwhile, trim the mushroom stems, rinse the mushrooms and pat dry. Melt the remaining butter in a nonstick 10-in (26-cm) sauté pan. Add the mushrooms and lemon juice, season with salt and pepper, and cook the mushrooms until they are golden and have stopped giving out any liquid.

❧ Add the pork, onions and mushrooms to the pot and cook over low heat, covered, for 1 hour longer.

❧ Remove the meat, pork, onions and mushrooms with a slotted spoon and set aside. Bring the sauce to boil. Blend the arrowroot and cold water, add to the boiling sauce and boil over high heat for 1½ minutes or until the sauce is thickened and smooth. Return the meat and other ingredients to the pot and reheat for 2 minutes. Transfer to a shallow dish and serve.

Serves 8

Ile-de-France

ENTRECÔTES BERCY, POMMES FRITES
RIB STEAKS BERCY STYLE, WITH FRENCH FRIES

The Bercy quarter of Paris, which for a long time was home to the most important wine market of Europe, gave its name to a method of cooking with wine and shallots that was fashionable in Parisian restaurants around 1820. This was also the era of the traveling marchands de frites *or* friteurs *who operated around the Pont-Neuf selling potatoes fried in sizzling hot oil called* pommes Pont-Neuf. *Gradually these merchants spread all over Paris and their fried potatoes became known simply as* frites *or* pommes frites.

2 lb (1 kg) boiling potatoes
about 2 qt (2 l) peanut (groundnut) oil
2 *entrecôtes,* rib steaks or Scotch fillets,
   1¼ lb (600 g) each, trimmed
salt and freshly ground pepper
6 tablespoons (3 oz/100 g) beef marrow
1 tablespoon vegetable oil
⅓ cup (3 oz/100 g) butter
4 French shallots, finely chopped
6 tablespoons (3 fl oz/90 ml) dry white wine
1 tablespoon chopped flat-leaf parsley

✤ Peel the potatoes, wash them and cut them into pieces 2–2½ in (5–6 cm) long and ½ in (1 cm) wide. Rinse under cold water and dry in a tea towel.

✤ Heat the oil in a deep fryer to 350°F (180°C). As soon as it starts to bubble, add the potatoes in a frying basket, in batches if necessary, and fry until a pale straw color. Remove the basket from the oil and set the fries aside; maintain the oil at 350°F (180°C).

✤ Pat the steaks dry and season with salt and pepper. Cut the beef marrow into ¼-in (.5-cm) cubes. Drop into a saucepan of simmering water and poach for 3 minutes. Drain the marrow in a sieve.

✤ Heat the oil in a nonstick 10-in (26-cm) skillet. Add 2 tablespoons butter. As soon as it melts, add the steaks and cook for 1½–2½ minutes on each side, according to taste. Remove from the pan and keep warm; discard the fat from the pan. Add the shallots and wine and cook over high heat, scraping up browned bits with a wooden spoon, until the liquid is reduced to 1 tablespoon. Remove the pan from the heat and whisk in the remaining butter in small pieces to make a light, foamy sauce. Add the parsley and pour over the steaks. Reheat the marrow in the skillet for 30 seconds and scatter over the meat.

✤ Plunge the basket of potatoes back into the hot oil and fry until crisp and golden brown. Drain on paper towels. Sprinkle with salt and turn onto a plate. Serve the steaks immediately, accompanied by the potatoes.

Serves 4

RIB STEAKS BERCY STYLE, WITH FRENCH FRIES

PEPPER STEAK

Ile-de-France

STEAK AU POIVRE
PEPPER STEAK

Invented around 1920 in the kitchens of the Trianon Palace at Versailles, steak au poivre has become one of the classic dishes of French cuisine. In order to give a lift to some very tender but rather tasteless beef from Argentina, the chef, Emile Lerch, had the idea of covering it with crushed peppercorns before cooking it. Today, mignonette or coarse ground pepper is also referred to as poivre à steak.

1 porterhouse or rump steak, about 13 oz (400 g) and 1 in (3 cm) thick
salt
1 tablespoon cracked peppercorns
¼ cup (2 oz/60 g) butter
2 tablespoons cognac
3 tablespoons heavy (double) cream or crème fraîche

♣ Ask the butcher to trim the meat and to cut it into two steaks of equal size. Pat dry and season with salt. Spread the peppercorns on a plate and roll the steaks over them to coat each side lightly.

♣ Melt half the butter in a 10-in (26-cm) skillet. Cook the steaks over high heat for 2–3 minutes on each side, according to taste. Pour the cognac over and ignite. When the flames subside, remove the steaks from the pan and keep warm on a plate.

♣ Discard the butter from the pan and add the cream. Boil for 1 minute over high heat, then whisk in the remaining butter.

♣ Pour this sauce over the steaks and serve immediately.

Serves 2

Bretagne

KIG-HA-FARZ
BUCKWHEAT PUDDING WITH MEAT AND VEGETABLES

This traditional Breton dish was once served at family celebrations. The woman of the house carefully kept the white linen bags in which the farz was enclosed, boiling and drying them in the sun after each use. They were then put away in the linen cupboard until the next occasion.

3 lb (1.5 kg) beef suitable for braising, such as top round (topside), neck or chuck
1 onion
3 cloves
1 lb (500 g) fresh pork belly
bouquet garni: 1 bay leaf, 1 sprig thyme, 6 sprigs parsley, 3 celery stalks (tied together)
1 tablespoon coarse sea salt
1 teaspoon mixed black and white peppercorns
½ teaspoon coriander seeds
3 leeks
1 green cabbage
6 carrots, peeled
6 turnips, peeled
1 celery heart
2 tablespoons butter
salt and freshly ground pepper

FOR THE *FARZ:*

¼ cup (2 oz/60 g) butter
1⅔ cups (8 oz/250 g) buckwheat flour
6 tablespoons (3 fl oz/90 ml) milk
6 tablespoons (3 fl oz/90 ml) heavy (double) cream or crème fraîche
1 egg
1 teaspoon superfine (caster) sugar
½ cup (3 oz/100 g) raisins

⚜ Pour 4 qt (4 l) water into a large pot and bring to boil. Add the piece of beef and simmer gently for 15 minutes, skimming the surface regularly. Peel the onion and stud with cloves. Add the pork belly, bouquet garni, onion, coarse salt, peppercorns and coriander to the pot, cover and simmer gently for 2 hours.

⚜ Trim off the deep green parts of the leeks. Wash the leeks and halve crosswise, separating the white part from the tender green part; tie together in two bundles. Quarter and core the cabbage.

⚜ To prepare the *farz:* transfer ¾ cup (6 fl oz/ 200 ml) of the cooking liquid from the pot to a small saucepan. Add the ¼ cup (2 oz/60 g) butter and allow it to melt. Sift the flour into a bowl. Add the butter mixture, milk, cream, egg and sugar and mix to a smooth paste using a wooden spoon. Blend in the raisins. Wrap the mixture in a square of white cotton cloth and tie the two ends with kitchen thread, taking care not to compress the *farz* too much.

⚜ Add the leeks, carrots, turnips and celery to the pot and return to boil. Add the *farz* and simmer gently for another 1½ hours.

⚜ Meanwhile, parboil the cabbage in water to cover for 5 minutes. Drain and transfer to a nonstick 10-in (26-cm) sauté pan with the 2 tablespoons butter. Season with salt and pepper. Cover and cook over very low heat for 1 hour or until very tender. Keep warm.

⚜ Remove the cooked vegetables, meats and *farz* from the pot and strain the stock into a soup tureen. Slice the meats and arrange on a plate; surround with vegetables. Remove the *farz* from its cloth covering and coarsely crumble it around the vegetables. Have guests help themselves to some of each, pouring a little of the stock over before eating.

Serves 6   *Photograph page 79*

PORK WITH PRUNES (TOP) AND PORK WITH CHESTNUTS (BOTTOM)

Périgord

PORC AUX CHÂTAIGNES

PORK WITH CHESTNUTS

1 pork fillet, about 2 lb (1 kg), boned and
    trimmed of fat
salt and freshly ground pepper
1 tablespoon vegetable oil
2 tablespoons butter
4 cloves garlic, peeled

3 tablespoons white vermouth
½ teaspoon sugar
6 tablespoons (3 fl oz/90 ml) water
1½ lb (750 g) chestnuts

❧ Ask the butcher to tie the pork fillet at
intervals. Season with salt and pepper.
❧ Heat the oil in an oval pot in which the meat
will fit comfortably. Add half the butter and
the garlic, and brown the meat on all sides.

❧ Remove the meat and garlic and discard the cooking fat. Add the vermouth and sugar, and boil over high heat until slightly reduced, scraping up browned bits with a wooden spoon. Return the meat to the pot and turn it over in the liquid. Add the garlic and water and bring to simmer. Cover and cook over low heat for 45 minutes, turning the meat over twice.

❧ Meanwhile, make a slash on the flat side of each chestnut. Bring a large saucepan of water to boil. Drop in the chestnuts and boil for 5 minutes. Drain, then shell and remove the brown skin that covers each chestnut.

❧ Add the chestnuts to the pot and cook for 45 minutes longer, turning both meat and chestnuts several times.

❧ When the meat is cooked, transfer it to a serving plate and surround with chestnuts. Add the remaining butter to the sauce in the pot and stir until it melts. Pour sauce over the chestnuts and serve immediately.

Serves 4

Périgord/Picardie

PORC AUX PRUNEAUX
PORK WITH PRUNES

1 pork fillet, about 2 lb (1 kg), boned and
    trimmed of fat
salt
1 bay leaf, crushed
30 prunes
8 walnuts
3 oz (100 g) lean bacon
2 French shallots, finely chopped
4 leaves dried sage
¼ cup (2 fl oz/60 ml) dry white wine
freshly ground pepper
1 tablespoon vegetable oil

❧ Ask the butcher to tie the pork fillet at intervals. Rub the salt and the bay leaf over the pork. Remove the pits from 10 prunes and chop them. Coarsely grate the nuts, using a cylindrical grater with large holes. Remove the rind from the bacon. Finely chop the bacon and cook with the shallots in a nonstick 9-in (22-cm) skillet, stirring often, until lightly browned, about 5 minutes. Remove from heat. Crumble in the sage leaves and add the pepper, grated walnuts, 1 tablespoon wine and the chopped prunes.

❧ Pit the remaining prunes, making a single slit in the side. Fill each with a small mound of the stuffing and close the prune over the stuffing. To stuff the roast, make two cuts through the center in the shape of an "X" and make shallow crisscross cuts over the whole surface of the meat. Stuff the meat with the remaining prune mixture, pushing it well in so that the stuffing is not visible from the outside.

❧ Lightly oil an oval baking dish just large enough to hold the pork surrounded by the stuffed prunes. Oil the meat and place it in the dish. Heat an oven to 425°F (215°C) and roast the pork for 30 minutes, then surround the meat with the prunes and pour the remaining wine over them. Reduce the heat to 375°F (190°C) and roast for 1 hour longer. Transfer the roast to a platter, surround with prunes and serve.

Serves 4

Ile-de-France

NAVARIN PRINTANIER

LAMB WITH SPRING VEGETABLES

On October 20, 1827, the French, English and Russian armies together defeated the Egyptian and Turkish fleet at Navarin in Greece in the course of the Greek War of Independence. It is thought that this dish of lamb stewed with vegetables was christened navarin *in honor of the war.*

3¼ lb (1.6 kg) lamb shoulder, neck and
    breast, mixed
salt and freshly ground pepper
6 oz (200 g) ripe tomatoes
1 tablespoon vegetable oil
3 tablespoons butter
1 tablespoon all-purpose (plain) flour
2 cups (16 fl oz/500 ml) chicken stock
    (recipe page 120)
bouquet garni: 1 bay leaf, 1 sprig thyme,
    6 sprigs parsley (tied together)
2 cloves garlic, halved
1 lb (500 g) fresh peas, in the shell
1 lb (500 g) very small carrots
1 lb (500 g) small turnips
18 small green (spring) onions
6 oz (200 g) slender green beans
1 teaspoon sugar
1 tablespoon chopped fresh chervil

❧ Cut the meat into 2-in (5-cm) cubes and season with salt and pepper. Drop the tomatoes into boiling water for 10 seconds. Cool under running water, then peel, halve, squeeze out the seeds and finely chop the flesh.

❧ Heat oil in a 4-qt (4-l) flameproof casserole, add half the butter and lightly brown the cubes of meat on all sides. Sprinkle with flour and cook, stirring, for 1 minute. Stir in the tomatoes, stock, bouquet garni and garlic. Cover and cook over low heat for 1½ hours.

❧ Meanwhile, prepare the vegetables: shell the peas. Peel the carrots and turnips. Peel the onions and cut off the green stalks. Remove the strings from the beans, if necessary, and blanch in a large quantity of boiling water for 5 minutes, then drain.

❧ Melt the remaining butter in a nonstick 11-in (28-cm) sauté pan. Add the carrots, turnips and onions and cook over low heat until lightly golden, about 5 minutes, stirring frequently. Add the beans and peas and sprinkle with sugar, salt and pepper. Cook until vegetables are golden, about 2 minutes longer. Add ¾ cup (6 fl oz/200 ml) of the lamb cooking liquid and simmer over low heat for 15 minutes.

❧ After the meat has cooked for 1½ hours, add the vegetables and cook over low heat, stirring, for 5 minutes. Remove the meat and vegetables with a slotted spoon, transfer to a shallow dish and keep warm. Boil the cooking liquid until thickened, then remove the garlic and bouquet garni. Stir in the chervil. Pour the sauce over the meat and vegetables and serve.

Serves 6   *Photograph page 66*

Bretagne

GIGOT D'AGNEAU À LA BRETONNE

LEG OF LAMB BRITTANY STYLE

Haricot beans, one of the best known vegetables from Bretagne, are the main ingredient of any dish called à la bretonne. *The beans may be left whole or puréed.*

LEG OF LAMB BRITTANY STYLE (LEFT) AND BUCKWHEAT PUDDING WITH MEAT AND VEGETABLES (RIGHT, RECIPE PAGE 74)

1 onion

2 cloves

6 cloves garlic

3 lb (1.5 kg) fresh haricot (white) beans, shelled

5 oz (150 g) carrots, peeled and coarsely chopped

bouquet garni: 1 bay leaf, 1 sprig thyme,
   6 sprigs parsley (tied together)

1 leg of lamb, about 3½ lb (1.7 kg), trimmed

2 tablespoons peanut (groundnut) oil

salt and freshly ground pepper

2 tablespoons butter

❧ Peel the onion and stud with cloves. Peel and halve 4 cloves of garlic.

❧ Combine the beans, onion, carrots, bouquet garni and halved garlic cloves in a large saucepan and cover with plenty of water. Bring to boil over low heat. Simmer gently for 1½ hours, seasoning with salt after 1 hour.

❧ When the beans have been cooking for 30 minutes, preheat an oven to 475°F (245°C). Peel the remaining 2 cloves of garlic and cut each into 6 slivers. Make incisions in the leg of lamb with the point of a knife and slip a sliver of garlic into each. Rub the lamb with oil and season with salt and pepper. Oil a large roasting pan and rack and place the leg of lamb on the rack, curved side down.

❧ Roast the lamb for 20 minutes, then turn it over, reduce heat to 450°F (230°C) and roast for 25 minutes longer, checking that the juices in the pan do not burn; they should only caramelize. If the juices begin to burn, add a few spoonfuls of water to the pan. A leg of lamb this size will be roasted to the rosy-pink stage in 45 minutes. Turn off the oven, turn the lamb over and let rest for 10 minutes.

❧ When the beans are cooked, drain them and discard the bouquet garni, onion and garlic. Discard the fat from the roasting pan and add the butter. Turn the beans into the pan and stir to coat with the butter and pan juices. Transfer to a serving dish. Place the leg of lamb on a platter and serve with the beans.

Serves 6

BRAISED BEEF WITH ANCHOVIES (TOP) AND CORSICAN STEW WITH PASTA (BOTTOM)

Languedoc

BROUFADO

BRAISED BEEF WITH ANCHOVIES

3 lb 10 oz (1.8 kg) rump steak
¼ cup (2 fl oz/60 ml) olive oil
¼ cup (2 fl oz/60 ml) red wine vinegar
2 cups (16 fl oz/500 ml) dry white wine
3 tablespoons cognac
2 onions, thinly sliced
2 cloves garlic, halved
bouquet garni: 1 sprig thyme, 1 bay leaf,
    6 sprigs parsley (tied together)
salt and freshly ground pepper
3 anchovies preserved in salt
3 tablespoons capers, rinsed and dried
4 cornichons (small French sour pickles or
    gherkins), thinly sliced
1 teaspoon arrowroot
2 tablespoons cold water

❧ Cut the meat into 2-in (5-cm) cubes. Pour 2 tablespoons oil, the vinegar, wine and cognac into a large bowl. Add the onions and meat and combine. Cover and refrigerate for 12 hours.

❧ Preheat an oven to 350°F (180°C). Pour the contents of the bowl into a 4-qt (4-l) pot. Add the garlic, bouquet garni, salt and pepper and bring to simmer. Cover and braise in the oven for 4 hours.

❧ Rub the salt off the anchovies under cold running water. Remove the fillets from the skin and cut in fourths. Add the capers and cornichons to the pot and braise for 1 hour longer.

❧ Transfer the pieces of meat to a warmed plate using a slotted spoon. Blend the arrowroot with the cold water and pour into the sauce. Boil until the mixture thickens, about 2 minutes. Stir in the anchovies, then return the meat to the pot and simmer for 5 minutes. Serve directly from the pot.

Serves 6

Corse

STUFATU

CORSICAN STEW WITH PASTA

Stufatu *is the Corsican word for stew. The term is applied to numerous dishes cooked by simmering.*

2½ lb (1.25 kg) beef suitable for braising, such as neck or chuck
8 oz (250 g) raw smoked ham
1 lb (500 g) ripe tomatoes
¼ cup (2 fl oz/60 ml) olive oil
3 onions, thinly sliced
6 cloves garlic, finely chopped
1 cup (8 fl oz/250 ml) dry white wine
bouquet garni: 1 bay leaf, 1 sprig thyme, 1 sprig rosemary, 6 sprigs parsley (tied together)
salt and freshly ground pepper

4 pinches freshly grated nutmeg
1 oz (30 g) dried *cèpes* (*porcini* mushrooms)

FOR SERVING:
12 oz (375 g) fresh pasta, or 10 oz (315 g) dried pasta
3 tablespoons butter
4 oz (100 g) Corsican sheep's milk cheese or Parmesan, freshly grated

❧ Cut the beef and ham into ¾-in (2-cm) cubes. Drop the tomatoes into boiling water for 10 seconds. Cool under running water, peel, halve and squeeze out the seeds; coarsely chop the flesh.

❧ Heat the oil in a 4-qt (4-l) pot and cook the beef, ham, onions and garlic for 5 minutes, stirring constantly with a wooden spoon. Add the tomatoes, wine and bouquet garni and mix well. Season with salt, pepper and nutmeg and bring to simmer. Cover and simmer for 1 hour.

❧ Meanwhile, place the mushrooms in a bowl, cover with 2 cups warm water and leave them to swell.

❧ Add the mushrooms to the pot with the strained soaking liquid and simmer them for 2 hours longer.

❧ To prepare the pasta: drop the pasta into a large pot of boiling salted water and cook until *al dente*. Drain, place in a shallow dish and toss with the butter. Pour over half the sauce from the meat and mix well. Season with pepper and serve the meat in its sauce accompanied by the pasta; pass the grated cheese separately.

Serves 6

Languedoc

CASSOULET

TOULOUSE CASSEROLE

The word cassoulet *comes from* cassole, *the name of the glazed earthenware dish in which the* cassoulet *is gratinéed. The main ingredient is haricot beans (originally brought to France from Spain in the sixteenth century), which must be local—from either Cazères or Pamiers—and must have been picked within the year. To these are added different meats, according to the area. This version is the simplest, and perhaps the oldest, and originated in Castelnaudary.*

1½ lb (750 g) dried haricot (white) beans
1 lb (500 g) lightly salted pork belly
8 oz (250 g) fresh pork rind, trimmed of all fat
1 lb (500 g) Toulouse (coarse-textured) sausage
1 unsmoked kielbasa (boiling sausage)
8 cloves garlic
1 teaspoon dried thyme
salt and freshly ground pepper
1½ lb (750 g) fresh pork tenderloin (fillet),
    bones removed and reserved
13 oz (400 g) ripe tomatoes
3 onions
2 cloves
2 leeks, white and tender green parts only,
    washed and thinly sliced
bouquet garni: 1 bay leaf, 1 sprig thyme,
    6 sprigs parsley (tied together)
¾ cup (6 oz/200 g) goose fat
3 tablespoons dried white breadcrumbs

❧ Place the beans in a pot and cover with plenty of cold water. Let soak for 4 hours.
❧ Parboil the pork belly and pork rind in water to cover for 5 minutes, then rinse and drain. Cut the pork rind into strips 1¼ in (3 cm) wide. Roll the strips over themselves and secure with kitchen thread. Prick the sausages with a fork to keep them from bursting during cooking.
❧ Peel 2 cloves of garlic and cut each into 6 slivers. Mix the thyme, salt, pepper and garlic slivers. Make 12 slits in the surface of the pork tenderloin and slip a piece of garlic into each.
❧ Drop the tomatoes into boiling water for 10 seconds. Cool under running water, peel, halve and squeeze out the seeds; coarsely chop the flesh. Peel 4 cloves of garlic and chop finely. Peel the onions; stud one with cloves and finely chop the remainder.
❧ Drain the beans, discarding the soaking water. Return them to the pot and cover with 3 qt (3 l) of cold water. Add the pork belly, leeks, clove-studded onion, bouquet garni, pork rind and the bone from the pork tenderloin and bring to boil over very low heat. Simmer for 1½ hours.
❧ Meanwhile, melt ⅓ cup (3 oz/100 g) goose fat in a heavy pot large enough to hold the tenderloin, and brown it on all sides. Remove and set aside. Add the chopped onions to the pot and cook over low heat until golden, about 5 minutes, stirring with a wooden spoon. Add the chopped garlic and cook, stirring, for 2 minutes. Add the tomatoes and cook for 3 minutes longer. Season with salt and pepper. Return the meat to the pot, cover and cook over low heat for 1 hour.
❧ Remove the meat and add it with the cooking liquid to the beans. Add the sausages and cook for 30 minutes longer.
❧ Preheat an oven to 375°F (190°C).

TOULOUSE CASSEROLE, PHOTOGRAPHED IN LANGUEDOC

Remove the meats from the pot and carve into ¼-in (.5-cm) slices. Remove the thread from the rolls of pork rind and cut them into 1¼- by ¼-in (3- by .5-cm) strips. Discard the onion and bouquet garni.

⚜ Halve the remaining 2 cloves of garlic and rub over the inside of a large casserole. Spread a layer of beans on the bottom; cover with a layer of mixed meats. Continue to layer the ingredients, finishing with a layer of beans. Melt the remaining goose fat and pour over the surface. Sprinkle with the breadcrumbs and bake for 1½ hours. Serve directly from the casserole.

Serves 8–10

VEGETABLES

FRANCE IS ONE LARGE GARDEN, lavishly planted from north to south. Large-scale farming, greenhouse culture, market gardens: these are the sources of some splendid ingredients.

There is nothing more agreeable than choosing one's vegetables at the *Marché d'Intérât National,* situated at Rungis. In this world of concrete and galvanized iron, the professional—restaurateur or wholesaler of fruit and vegetables—comes in search of the best of the best. Purple artichokes from Provence, cabbages from Alsace and Auvergne, endives from Flanders, beans from Poitou, broad beans from Aquitaine, peas from Vendée, potatoes from Ile-de-France: all are here, according to season, and they do not even begin to exhaust the enormous richness of the French vegetable garden.

Each vegetable speaks for a region. The zucchini, pepper and olive evoke the markets of Provence and the Côte d'Azur. The market of Forville, at Cannes, bears witness to the abundance of this land of sunshine. Brittany has elected as king and queen the artichoke and the potato. The sweet pepper is the glory of the Basque village Espelette. And if beets belong to the north, cardoons—fine-flavored but stringy cousins of the artichoke that are eaten as a gratin and with beef marrow—are part of the territory of Lyons.

The noble asparagus is found as readily in Sologne, at Vineuil, as it is in the Lubéron at Pertuis, in Alsace at Village-Neuf or Hoerdt, in the Val de Loire near Chinon. Anyone willing to trade it for the "common" leek would be delighted to discover that the latter is, in fact, just as rich in possibilities as its better-born neighbor.

Cabbage is a vegetable with a thousand uses. Artichokes are equally good stewed *à la barigoule,* in vinaigrette or garnishing a *pâté de foie gras.* Or a combination of vegetables—a bouquet of peas, baby carrots, onions, turnips and green beans epitomizes spring; ratatouille and exquisitely stuffed vegetables symbolize Provence. Vegetables may be eaten as fritters, pan-fried, flavored with onion, garlic, fresh herbs, butter or oil; they may be fried, roasted, simmered, braised—in a *bain-marie,* in a cast-iron casserole, in the oven.

Alone, vegetables might constitute a whole meal: witness the *truffade* of Auvergne; a dish of lentils enriched with cubes of salt pork, or cabbage filled with a succulent stuffing. In countless traditional dishes, vegetables are the central element; they give the dish its flavor, its unity, its *raison d'être.* In the Middle Ages they were somewhat neglected, and the nineteenth century practically smothered them under a heap of over-refined sauces. Nouvelle cuisine has restored vegetables to a position of honor.

AUVERGNE-STYLE LENTILS (LEFT, RECIPE PAGE **89**) AND
STUFFED MUSHROOMS (RIGHT, RECIPE PAGE **89**)

Languedoc

POMMES SARLADAISES
POTATOES SARLAT STYLE

1½ lb (750 g) boiling potatoes
3 tablespoons goose fat
4 cloves garlic, finely chopped
2 tablespoons chopped flat-leaf parsley
salt and freshly ground pepper

❧ Peel the potatoes, wash and slice into ⅛-in (3-mm) rounds.

❧ Melt the goose fat in a nonstick 10-in (26-cm) skillet. Add the potatoes and turn them over in the hot fat for 10 minutes. Add the garlic and parsley, season with salt and pepper and stir again. Cover and cook over low heat for 20 minutes or until the potatoes are tender, turning them several times.

❧ Transfer the potatoes to a shallow dish and serve hot.

Serves 4

Savoie

GRATIN SAVOYARD
POTATO GRATIN SAVOY STYLE

1¼ cups (10 fl oz/300 ml) chicken stock (recipe page 120)
salt and freshly ground pepper
6 pinches freshly grated nutmeg
1¼ lb (625 g) boiling potatoes
2½ tablespoons butter
4 oz (125 g) Beaufort or Emmenthaler cheese, freshly and finely grated

❧ Preheat an oven to 375°F (190°C). Bring the chicken stock to boil in a saucepan over low heat. Add salt, pepper and nutmeg and remove from heat.

❧ Peel the potatoes, wash them and pat dry. Using the shredder attachment of a food processor, slice the potatoes very thinly.

❧ Using a small amount of the butter, grease a 10- by 7-in (26- by 18-cm) baking dish. Spread a layer of potatoes over the bottom, then a layer of cheese. Continue layering the remaining potatoes and cheese, ending with cheese. Pour the hot stock over and dot with the remaining butter.

❧ Bake until golden brown, about 50 minutes. Serve hot from the baking dish.

Serves 4

Provence

BARBOUIADO DE FÈVES ET D'ARTICHAUTS
BRAISED BROAD BEANS AND ARTICHOKES

3 lb (1.5 kg) fresh broad beans
3 oz (100 g) streaky bacon
5 small artichokes, about 4 oz (125 g) each
½ lemon
2 tablespoons olive oil
1 green onion (scallion or spring onion), finely chopped
1 sprig thyme
1 sprig savory
3 tablespoons water
salt and freshly ground pepper

POTATO GRATIN SAVOY STYLE (TOP LEFT), POTATOES SARLAT STYLE (BOTTOM)
AND BRAISED BROAD BEANS AND ARTICHOKES (RIGHT)

✤ Shell the broad beans and peel off the soft green skin from each bean. Remove the rind from the bacon and cut the meat into thin matchsticks.

✤ Trim each artichoke stalk at the base of the heart. Remove the tough outside leaves. Cut off the tips of the tender leaves to within ¼ in (½ cm) of the heart. Trim the hearts and rub with the cut surface of the lemon. Cut each heart into quarters and remove the choke. Cut each quarter into 3 slices.

✤ Heat the oil in a 4-qt (4-l) pot. Add the onion, bacon, thyme and savory and cook gently for 2 minutes, stirring with a wooden spoon. Add the artichokes and cook over moderate heat, stirring constantly, until light golden and almost tender, about 7–8 minutes.

✤ Add the water and beans and season with salt and pepper. Mix well. Cover and cook for 5 minutes longer. Remove from heat and discard the thyme and savory. Turn into a shallow dish and serve immediately.

Serves 4

GREEN PEAS VENDÉE STYLE

Vendée

PETITS POIS À LA VENDÉENNE
GREEN PEAS VENDÉE STYLE

1 sprig thyme
1 sprig hyssop
1 sprig savory
1 sprig flat-leaf parsley
3 tablespoons butter
16 fresh green onions (scallions or spring
    onions)
3 lb (1.5 kg) green peas, shelled
2 lettuce hearts, quartered
salt and freshly ground pepper
1 teaspoon sugar

❧ Strip the leaves from the thyme, hyssop, savory and parsley.

❧ Melt the butter in a nonstick 10-in (26-cm) sauté pan. Add the onions and herbs and cook over low heat, stirring, for 3 minutes or until the onions are golden. Add the peas and cook, stirring, for 2 minutes longer. Add the lettuce hearts, season with salt, pepper and sugar and add cold water just to cover.

❧ Cover the pan and cook for 1 hour, stirring from time to time. Turn the peas into a shallow dish and serve immediately.

Serves 4

Vendée

EMBEURRÉE DE CHOU
BUTTERED CABBAGE

1 white cabbage, about 2 lb (1 kg)
⅓ cup (3 oz/100 g) butter
salt and freshly ground pepper

❧ Remove the large outside leaves of the cabbage, then cook the cabbage in a large pot of boiling water for 10 minutes. Drain, cut into quarters and remove the hard core. Cut each quarter into very fine strips, cutting away the hard ribs.

❧ Melt half the butter in a nonstick 11-in (28-cm) sauté pan. Add the cabbage, season with salt and pepper and cook for about 20 minutes or until the cabbage is very soft. Remove from heat, add the remaining butter and stir well, mashing the cabbage slightly.

❧ Turn the buttered cabbage into a shallow bowl and serve immediately.

Serves 4   *Photograph page 90*

Périgord

CÈPES FARCIS
STUFFED MUSHROOMS

12 large fresh *cèpes* (*porcini* mushrooms)
3 tablespoons olive oil
3½ oz (100 g) prosciutto or other raw ham,
   finely chopped
3½ oz (100 g) *ventrèche, pancetta* or rindless
   bacon, chopped
2 cloves garlic, finely chopped
2 French shallots, finely chopped
2 tablespoons chopped flat-leaf parsley
salt and freshly ground pepper
2 eggs, beaten

❧ Remove the stems of the mushrooms and trim off the base. Quickly wash the caps and stems under cold running water and pat dry. Finely chop the stems.

❧ Heat 1 tablespoon oil in a nonstick 10-in (26-cm) skillet and cook the ham and *ventrèche* for 2 minutes, stirring. Add the garlic and shallots and cook for 2 more minutes, stirring. Add the chopped mushroom stems and parsley and cook until golden. Remove from heat. Season lightly with salt and pepper. Add the eggs and mix well.

❧ Preheat an oven to 400°F (200°C). Lightly oil a baking dish large enough to hold the mushroom caps in one layer. Arrange the caps upside down in the dish and fill with the stuffing. Sprinkle with the remaining oil. Bake for 25 minutes or until the mushrooms are tender and the stuffing is golden brown. Arrange on a platter and serve immediately.

Serves 4   *Photograph page 84*

Auvergne

LENTILLES À L'AUVERGNATE
AUVERGNE-STYLE LENTILS

3 carrots
3 onions
2 cloves
2 cloves garlic, crushed
1 lb (500 g) lentils
7 oz (200 g) smoked bacon, in one piece
bouquet garni: 1 bay leaf, 1 sprig thyme,
   6 sprigs parsley (tied together)
2 tablespoons lard
1 tablespoon chopped flat-leaf parsley
1 tablespoon chopped fresh chives
salt and freshly ground pepper

❧ Cut the carrots into ¼-in (.5-cm) slices. Peel the onions; stud one onion with cloves and finely chop the remainder.

❧ Rinse the lentils, then place in a large pot. Add the bacon, whole onion, garlic, carrots and bouquet garni. Cover with cold water and bring to boil over low heat. Cook for 45 minutes.

❧ Lift out the bacon, remove the rind and fat and break the lean meat into small pieces. Melt the lard in a nonstick 10-in (26-cm) skillet and cook the chopped onions until golden, about 3 minutes, stirring with a wooden spoon. Add the bacon and cook, stirring, for 2 more minutes. Drain the lentils and discard the whole onion, garlic and bouquet garni. Stir in the contents of the skillet with the parsley and chives. Season with salt and pepper. Turn the lentils into a shallow dish and serve immediately.

Serves 6   *Photograph page 84*

Flandres

ENDIVES À LA FLAMANDE

ENDIVES FLEMISH STYLE

The endive is a vegetable from Belgium, which first appeared in France in 1879. It also goes by the names "Brussels chicory" and chicon.

2 lb (1 kg) Belgian endives (witloof or chicory)
3 tablespoons butter
1 tablespoon sugar
salt and freshly ground pepper
¼ cup (2 fl oz/60 ml) fresh lemon juice

❧ Pull off the outside leaves of the endives and the bitter part of the heart. Rinse the endives and pat dry.

❧ Preheat an oven to 400°F (200°C). Using a small amount of the butter, grease a baking dish large enough to hold the endives in a single layer. Arrange them in the dish, season with sugar, salt and pepper, and sprinkle with lemon juice. Dot with the remaining butter.

❧ Bake for 45 minutes or until soft and caramelized, turning the endives over halfway through cooking. Arrange on a platter and serve immediately.

Serves 4

Provence

HARICOTS VERTS À L'AIL

GREEN BEANS WITH GARLIC

1½ lb (750 g) young, very slender green beans
2 tablespoons extra virgin olive oil
6 cloves garlic, minced
2 tablespoons dried white breadcrumbs
2 tablespoons chopped flat-leaf parsley
salt and freshly ground pepper
2 tablespoons butter

❧ Drop the beans into a large pot of boiling salted water and cook uncovered over high heat for 6–8 minutes or until slightly crisp. Drain the beans in a colander, then drop them immediately into a large quantity of very cold water so that they retain their bright green color. Drain.

❧ Heat the oil in a nonstick 10-in (26-cm) sauté pan over low heat. Add the garlic, breadcrumbs, parsley and salt and pepper and cook, stirring, for 1 minute. Add the butter and, when it has melted, add the beans and stir to reheat. Serve immediately.

Serves 4

GREEN BEANS WITH GARLIC (TOP LEFT), BUTTERED CABBAGE (TOP RIGHT, RECIPE PAGE 88) AND ENDIVES FLEMISH STYLE (BOTTOM)

STUFFED CABBAGE (TOP, RECIPE PAGE 94) AND POTATO CREAM PIE (BOTTOM)

Bourbonnais

TRUFFAT
POTATO CREAM PIE

2 cups (10 oz/300 g) all-purpose (plain) flour
⅔ cup (5 oz/150 g) butter
¼ cup (2 fl oz/60 ml) water
salt
5 oz (150 g) smoked bacon
1 tablespoon peanut (groundnut) oil
1 large onion, finely chopped
1 lb 10 oz (800 g) boiling potatoes
freshly ground pepper
6 pinches freshly grated nutmeg
1 egg yolk

1 tablespoon milk
⅔ cup (5 oz/150 ml) heavy (double) cream
  or crème fraîche

❧ Sift the flour onto a work surface and make a well in the center. Add the butter, water and 3 pinches of salt. Combine the ingredients with the fingertips to produce a smooth dough. Roll it into a ball and refrigerate for 1 hour.
❧ Meanwhile, remove the rind from the bacon and chop the meat finely with a knife. Heat the oil in a nonstick 9-in (22-cm) skillet and cook the onion and bacon over low heat until golden, stirring with a wooden spoon. Remove from heat.

❧ Wash the potatoes and slice thinly. Turn into a bowl and add salt, pepper, nutmeg, and the mixture from the skillet. Combine carefully so that the potato slices do not break.

❧ Preheat an oven to 425°F (215°C). Cut the pastry into two portions, one slightly larger than the other. Roll out the larger portion to a 12-in (30-cm) circle. Butter a 10-in (26-cm) cake pan and line with pastry. Turn the potato mixture into the pastry case and smooth the surface. Roll out the second portion of pastry into a 10-in (26-cm) circle for the lid. Place on top of the filling and press the edges together firmly to seal.

❧ Beat together the egg yolk and milk and brush the surface of the pastry with this mixture. Bake for 1¼ hours or until the pastry is light golden. Cut a ¾-in (2-cm) circle of pastry from the center of the lid and pour the cream through this opening. Replace the circle of pastry and return the *truffat* to the oven for 10 minutes longer. Serve hot.

Serves 6

Provence

BEIGNETS DE LEGUMES
VEGETABLE FRITTERS

FOR THE BATTER:
1 cup (5 oz/150 g) all-purpose (plain) flour
salt
⅔ cup (5 fl oz/150 ml) milk
1 tablespoon olive oil
2 eggs, separated

FOR THE VEGETABLES:
1 eggplant (aubergine), about 5 oz (150 g)

1 zucchini (courgette), about 5 oz (150 g)
6 zucchini (courgette) flowers
2 artichokes, about 4 oz (125 g) each
½ lemon

FOR COOKING:
3 cups (24 fl oz/750 ml) peanut (groundnut) oil

❧ To prepare the fritter batter: sift the flour into a bowl. Whisk in the salt, milk and oil, then the egg yolks, whisking until the batter is smooth and homogeneous. Cover and let rest for 2 hours.

❧ After this time, prepare the vegetables: cut the eggplant and zucchini diagonally into ¼-in (.5-cm) slices. Remove the stamens from the zucchini flowers and cut each flower into 2 or 3 pieces, according to size. Break off the stalk of the artichokes level with the heart. Remove the tough outside leaves and cut off the tips of the tender leaves to within ½ in (1 cm) of the heart. Remove the chokes and rub the hearts with the lemon half to keep them from discoloring. Slice each artichoke vertically and sprinkle with lemon juice.

❧ Beat the egg whites to stiff peaks and fold into the batter. Heat the oil in a small deep fryer or saucepan to 375°F (190°C). Dip the artichoke, eggplant and zucchini slices and the zucchini flowers into the batter, then drop into the hot oil a few at a time and fry for 1–2 minutes or until golden brown.

❧ Remove the fritters with a slotted spoon and drain on paper towels. Arrange on a plate and serve immediately.

Serves 4   *Photograph pages 4–5*

Auvergne

CHOU FARCI

STUFFED CABBAGE

1 Savoy cabbage, about 3 lb (1.5 kg)
1 tablespoon vegetable oil
2 cloves garlic, finely chopped
2 French shallots, finely chopped
6 tablespoons (3 fl oz/90 ml) milk
2 oz (50 g) soft bread, crusts trimmed
13 oz (400 g) beef round steak (top round)
   or porterhouse
13 oz (400 g) fresh pork shoulder, boned and
   trimmed of fat
6 oz (200 g) fresh pork belly, boned
1 egg
2 tablespoons finely chopped mixed fresh
   parsley and chives
½ teaspoon dried thyme
½ teaspoon *quatre-épices* (see glossary)
salt and freshly ground pepper
1 sheet pork caul fat *(crépine)*
2 tablespoons butter
2 onions, thinly sliced
2 carrots, peeled and thinly sliced
bouquet garni: 1 bay leaf, 1 sprig thyme,
   10 sprigs parsley (tied together)
1 cup (8 fl oz/250 ml) chicken stock
   (recipe page 120)

❧ Remove the tough outer leaves from the cabbage and parboil the cabbage for 10 minutes in water to cover. Drain and let cool.

❧ Heat oil in a nonstick 8-in (20-cm) skillet and cook the garlic and shallots until golden. Pour the milk into a small saucepan and bring to boil. Crumble in the bread, remove from heat and stir to form a smooth paste. Let cool.

❧ Grind (mince) the three meats in a grinder or food processor. Add the garlic and bread mixtures, egg, herbs, *quatre-épices,* salt and pepper and mix well.

❧ To stuff the cabbage, stand it on its base and delicately spread the outside leaves, taking care not to tear them; as each leaf is spread out, cut away the thick white stalk from the base with a small knife. Continue in this way to the heart of the cabbage. Place half the stuffing in the heart. Fold the leaves back over the heart, adding a few spoonfuls of stuffing between the leaves. Use the last layer of leaves to cover the whole cabbage. Rinse the caul fat under cold water, drain and use it to wrap the cabbage.

❧ Preheat an oven to 425°F (215°C). Melt the butter in a heavy pot just large enough to hold the cabbage. Cook the onions and carrots until golden, stirring with a wooden spoon, about 5 minutes. Add the bouquet garni, salt, pepper and stock. Place the cabbage on top and cover. Bake for 1½ hours undisturbed.

❧ Transfer the cabbage to a platter. Strain the cooking liquid into a sauceboat. Quarter the cabbage, pour the sauce over and serve.

Serves 8   *Photograph page 92*

FLEURS DE COURGETTE FARCIES
STUFFED ZUCCHINI FLOWERS

18 large zucchini (courgette) flowers
8 oz (250 g) fresh sheep's milk cheese
grated rind of 1 lemon
⅓ cup (1½ oz/40 g) dried breadcrumbs
½ cup (2 oz/50 g) freshly and finely grated
   Parmesan cheese
2 tablespoons chopped flat-leaf parsley
salt and freshly ground pepper
2 egg whites
2½ tablespoons butter

❧ Preheat an oven to 425°F (215°C). Butter a 13- by 9-in (32- by 22-cm) baking dish. Remove the stamens from the zucchini flowers without destroying their shape or separating the petals. Wipe the flowers with a dampened cloth and set aside.

❧ Using a fork, mash the fresh cheese in a bowl. Add the lemon rind, breadcrumbs, half the Parmesan and the parsley. Season the cheese mixture liberally with salt and pepper and combine well.

❧ Beat the egg whites to stiff peaks and fold into the cheese mixture. Fill each flower with a portion of this mixture and roll up tightly to seal.

❧ Arrange the stuffed flowers in the baking dish. Melt the butter in a small saucepan and pour over the flowers. Sprinkle with the remaining Parmesan. Bake for 15 minutes or until the flowers have puffed up and become golden. Serve immediately.

Serves 6   *Photograph pages 4–5*

TIAN DE COURGETTES
BAKED ZUCCHINI WITH TOMATOES AND ONIONS

Tian *is the name of the square or rectangular glazed earthenware dish in which vegetable, meat or fish dishes are baked. Because of this, all Provençal gratins are called* tians.

1 lb (500 g) green (spring) onions
1 lb 10 oz (800 g) zucchini (courgettes)
1½ lb (750 g) firm-ripe tomatoes
6 tablespoons (3 fl oz/90 ml) olive oil
2 cloves garlic, finely chopped
salt and freshly ground pepper
1 sprig fresh thyme, leaves only
1 sprig fresh savory, leaves only (optional)

❧ Cut the onions into ¼-in (.5-cm) slices, including the green stalk. Cut the zucchini diagonally into ¼-in (.5-cm) slices; cut the tomatoes into similar-size slices.

❧ Preheat an oven to 400°F (200°C). Heat 4 tablespoons oil in a nonstick 10-in (26-cm) skillet and cook the onions over low heat, stirring frequently, until soft and transparent, about 8 minutes. Add garlic, salt and pepper and cook, stirring, for 2 minutes longer.

❧ Transfer the mixture to a 10- by 7-in (26- by 18-cm) baking dish and smooth the surface. Arrange 4 lengthwise rows of tomato and zucchini slices on top of the onions. Sprinkle with thyme and savory. Pour the remaining oil over and season with salt and pepper.

❧ Bake until the vegetables are very soft and slightly browned, about 1 hour. Serve directly from the baking dish, hot or lukewarm.

Serves 4–5   *Photograph pages 4–5*

Provence

ARTICHAUTS À LA BARIGOULE

BRAISED ARTICHOKES

Artichokes came to France with Catherine de' Medici. At first they were served simply grilled, like mushrooms. Barigoulo, the name of a mushroom in the Provençal dialect, is a recipe that has evolved into this fragrant sauté, which still goes by the original name.

12 young artichokes, about 4 oz (125 g) each
1 lemon, halved
¼ cup (2 fl oz/60 ml) olive oil
4 large onions, finely chopped
3 small carrots, peeled and thinly sliced
3 cloves garlic, cut into fine slivers
1 sprig thyme, crumbled
1 bay leaf
6 tablespoons (3 fl oz/90 ml) dry white wine
6 tablespoons (3 fl oz/90 ml) water
salt and freshly ground pepper

❧ Trim the artichoke stalks ¾ in (2 cm) from the heart and strip off the tough leaves. Cut off the tips of the tender leaves to within ¾ in (2 cm) of the heart. Pare the heart and stalks and rub with lemon.

❧ Heat the oil in an enameled pot just large enough to hold the artichokes. Add the onions and carrots and cook for 5 minutes without allowing them to color. Add the garlic and cook, stirring, for 1 minute longer.

❧ Rinse the artichokes and pat dry. Add to the pot with the thyme and bay leaf and cook, stirring, for 2 minutes. Add the wine and water and season with salt and pepper. Cover and cook over very low heat for about 1 hour or until the artichokes are easily pierced with a knife and are coated with a reduced sauce. Serve warm.

Serves 4

Aquitaine

CÈPES À LA BORDELAISE

CÈPES BORDELAISE STYLE

1½ lb (750 g) small fresh *cèpes* (porcini mushrooms)
¼ cup (2 fl oz/60 ml) olive oil
2 cloves garlic, finely chopped
3 tablespoons chopped flat-leaf parsley
salt and freshly ground pepper

❧ Cut off the stalks of the *cèpes* at the level of the cap. Quickly wash the caps under running water and pat dry.

❧ Heat the oil in a nonstick 10-in (26-cm) sauté pan over high heat. Add the *cèpes;* they will immediately give out a lot of liquid. Cook over very high heat, stirring constantly, until all liquid evaporates. Remove the *cèpes.* Add the garlic and parsley to the pan and cook, stirring, for 2 minutes, then turn out of the pan onto a plate.

❧ Return the *cèpes* to the pan, rounded surface up. Sprinkle with the garlic and parsley and season with salt and pepper. Cover and cook over low heat for 30 minutes.

❧ Arrange the *cèpes* on a serving plate. Boil the pan juices until reduced to a syrupy consistency. Pour over the *cèpes* and serve immediately.

Serves 4

CÈPES BORDELAISE STYLE (TOP) AND
BRAISED ARTICHOKES (BOTTOM)

DESSERTS

Brillat-Savarin deemed cheeses the *premier des desserts,* the most important. But in France, cheeses in all their diversity ("a country with four hundred different cheeses will never die," promised Churchill in 1940) remain a prelude to dessert.

The markets of eastern France feel the influence of central Europe, with Vienna at its hub, where cafes are meeting places. The town of Metz, for example, has one of the best chocolatiers in the whole country, Pierre Koenig, who exports his chocolate truffles, pralines and semisweet chocolate creams around the world. Metz is also home to a dozen or so top quality *pâtisseries-salons de thé.* Strasbourg is one of the most deliciously sweet towns in the world. Its specialties include *kugelhopf, büeraweka* (a fruit loaf), fruity Bettelmann cake, and *schnecke,* known in the rest of France as *pain aux raisins.* Many of the pâtisserie specialties of eastern France have spread to other parts of the country: the *meringue chantilly,* meringue with whipped cream, which is also found in Ile-de-France, for example.

Other regions have their own specialties, which rely on local resources: for example, in Brittany they are *kouigh amann au miel; prune-studded *far;* the rich butter cake known as *quatre-quarts;* and *galettes,* pastries made with salted butter. The *clafoutis* is now found everywhere, although it originated in the Limousin. The *baba*—a native of Lorraine?—becomes *savarin* when served in Paris, garnished with whipped cream.

Ice cream, introduced to the French court by Catherine de' Medici, who married the future Henri II in the sixteenth century, did not properly arrive in Paris until the following century, when Francesco Procopio opened the first cafe in Paris. This frozen treat—which became based on cream and eggs only around 1775—and sorbets, made from all kinds of fruit, were an immediate hit. In the eighteenth century, Paris had 250 *limonadiers* selling ice creams during summer.

Modern nutritional science has endorsed the serving of sorbets—an ancient Chinese practice, passed on to the Persians and Arabs—which use neither eggs nor fats. Based on fruit pulp, preferably fresh, sorbets calmly follow the rhythm of the changing seasons.

Tarts, too, wed the fruits of all regions, all seasons. *Crêpes* are not necessarily Breton, as evidenced by the very Parisian *crêpes Suzette,* delicately flavored with orange zest and dramatically flamed at the table. The dessert that finishes the meal should also be a feast for the eyes, hence the importance given to presentation. The great chefs have always understood that if the dinner does not climax in dessert, even the finest cuisine will be a disappointment, and that the dessert will never be complete unless it is properly presented.

WARM PRUNE TART (LEFT, RECIPE PAGE 101) AND
BUTTERED PASTRY (RIGHT, RECIPE PAGE 101)

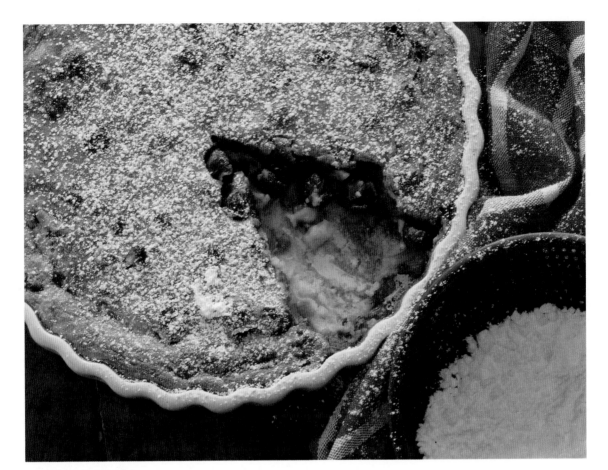

BAKED CHERRY CUSTARD

Limousin

CLAFOUTIS

BAKED CHERRY CUSTARD

The origin of the clafoutis is not known, but both Limousin and Auvergne—where the very similar millard is made—claim it as their own.

1½ lb (750 g) ripe black cherries, not pitted
2 eggs
1 egg yolk
½ cup (4 oz/125 g) sugar
5 tablespoons (2½ oz/75 g) butter, melted
½ cup (2½ oz/75 g) all-purpose (plain) flour
1 cup (8 fl oz/250 ml) milk
vanilla sugar or powdered (icing) sugar

❧ Preheat an oven to 400°F (200°C). Wash, dry and stem the cherries.

❧ Butter an ovenproof china or glazed earthenware mold large enough to hold the cherries in a single layer. Place the cherries in it. Combine the eggs and yolk in a bowl, add the sugar and whisk until the mixture is pale in color. Whisk in the butter. Sift in the flour and mix well, then mix in the milk. Beat until batter is smooth, then pour over the cherries.

✤ Bake for 40 minutes or until browned. Remove the *clafoutis* from the oven and sprinkle with vanilla sugar. Serve lukewarm, from the baking dish.

Serves 6

Bretagne

KOUIGH AMANN
BUTTERED PASTRY

The Douarnenez region is the home of this cake, whose name means bread and butter.

¾ cup plus 2 tablespoons (7½ oz/220 g) low-salt butter
10 oz (300 g) bread dough (recipe page 121)
1 cup (7 oz/220 g) plus 2 tablespoons superfine (caster) sugar

✤ Place the butter in a deep plate and work it with a fork until it is soft and the same consistency as the dough. Roll out the dough on a work surface into a square ⅜ in (1 cm) thick. Spread with butter to within ¾ in (2 cm) of the edges; sprinkle with 1 cup sugar. Fold the dough in thirds one way, then in thirds the other way. Roll it out as thinly as possible, being careful not to let any of the butter or sugar escape. Fold the pastry again, as before.
✤ Butter a 10-in (26-cm) cake pan. Lay the dough in it and push down gently with your fingers, taking care not to break it. Start from the center and work outward until the whole pan is covered with an even thickness of dough. Let rise for 30 minutes, preheating an oven to 425°F (200°C) after 10 minutes of

rising. Bake the tart for 35 minutes, basting with the butter that rises to the surface during the last 15 minutes of baking.
✤ Sprinkle the tart with the remaining 2 tablespoons sugar. Let cool slightly, then turn it out and serve.

Serves 6   *Photograph page 98*

Bretagne

FAR
WARM PRUNE TART

This is one of the most popular of Bretagne's desserts. It is served in different ways according to the region—plain in Saint Pol de Léon, filled with prunes at Quiberon, and with raisins at Brest.

11 oz (350 g) prunes
2 cups (16 fl oz/500 ml) milk
3 eggs
½ cup (4 oz/125 g) sugar
½ cup (2½ oz/75 g) all-purpose (plain) flour

✤ Soak the prunes in warm water to cover for 2 hours. Preheat an oven to 400°F (200°C). Heat the milk in a small saucepan over gentle heat. Combine the eggs and sugar in a bowl and whisk until the mixture is pale in color. Whisk in the flour, then the milk.
✤ Butter a 10-in (26-cm) deep-sided oven-proof tart plate. Drain the prunes and arrange in the plate. Cover with the batter and bake for about 45 minutes or until browned. Let tart cool slightly. Serve warm from the baking dish.

Serves 6   *Photograph page 98*

Provence

OREILLETTES
PASTRY PUFFS

Oreillettes *in Provence,* bottereaux *in Vendée,* bugnes *in Lyon,* frivolles *in Champagne—these are names for the fritters that are made all over France for Mardi Gras, mid-Lent, Christmas, and at times of family celebration.*

2 cups (10 oz/300 g) all-purpose (plain) flour
3 eggs
2 tablespoons soft butter
grated rind of 1 orange and 1 lemon
1 teaspoon orangeflower water
3 pinches salt
2 qt (2 l) peanut (groundnut) oil
superfine (caster) sugar

⚜ Sift the flour onto a work surface and make a well in the center. Add the eggs, butter, grated rinds, orangeflower water and salt and mix with your fingertips, beginning from the center and working out. Then work the dough by pushing it away from you repeatedly with the flat of your hand until it is smooth and soft and comes away from your fingers.
⚜ Roll the dough into a ball, wrap in plastic and refrigerate for 4 hours.
⚜ Roll the dough out on a floured surface as thinly as possible. Cut into 3- by 1½-in (8- by 4-cm) rectangles. Heat the oil in a deep fryer to 375°F (190°C). Drop in the dough pieces in batches and fry until puffed and brown. Drain on paper towels. Pile the pastries on a plate, sprinkling sugar over each layer. They should be served the day they are made.

Makes 20–30   *Photograph page 6*

Ile-de-France

CRÊPES SUZETTE
ORANGE LIQUEUR CRÊPES

Were these famous pancakes invented in 1896 at the Café de Paris when the Prince of Wales visited in the company of a lady named Suzette, or in 1898 at the Maire restaurant? The mystery remains. For their filling, some people maintain that mandarin oranges are indispensable; others prefer oranges.

FOR THE BATTER:
¾ cup (4 oz/125 g) all-purpose (plain) flour
2 cups (16 fl oz/500 ml) milk
2 eggs
1 tablespoon sugar
1 envelope vanilla sugar or 3 drops vanilla extract (essence)
1 tablespoon peanut (groundnut) oil
4 pinches salt
½ cup (4 oz/125 g) soft butter

FOR THE GARNISH:
2 mandarin oranges
⅓ cup (3 oz/90 g) sugar
3 tablespoons cognac
6 tablespoons (3 fl oz/90 ml) curaçao

⚜ To prepare the batter: place the flour in a food processor. Add the milk, eggs, sugar and vanilla sugar, oil and salt and process until you have a smooth, liquid batter. Pour through a strainer into a bowl and let rest for 1 hour.
⚜ Melt 1½ tablespoons butter in a nonstick 8-in (22-cm) skillet, then pour it into a bowl. Using a small ladle, pour some batter into the skillet and tilt it so that the mixture covers the bottom. When it is golden on the bottom, after about 40 seconds, turn the crêpe over with a

spatula and cook for about 30 seconds longer.

❧ Ten minutes before serving, wash the mandarin oranges and wipe dry. Grate the rind finely into the skillet in which the crêpes were cooked. Halve the oranges and squeeze the juice into the skillet. Add the remaining butter, the sugar, 1 tablespoon cognac and 3 tablespoons curaçao and boil until a thick syrup forms, about 1 minute. Dip the crêpes into the syrup one by one, fold each in quarters and arrange on a large plate; keep warm. Drizzle with the syrup remaining in the skillet.

❧ Heat the remaining cognac and curaçao in a small saucepan. Bring the crêpes to the table. Pour the boiling alcohol mixture over them and ignite. Serve as soon as the flames subside.

Serves 6   *Photograph pages 108–109*

Ile-de-France

CRÈME CARAMEL
VANILLA CUSTARD WITH CARAMEL SAUCE

This family dessert is sometimes made without the caramel, in which case it goes by the name of oeufs au lait *(eggs with milk).*

1 vanilla bean (pod)
1 qt (1 l) whole milk
¾ cup (6½ oz/200 g) sugar
½ teaspoon fresh lemon juice
2 tablespoons water
8 eggs

❧ Preheat an oven to 350°F (180°C). Split vanilla bean in two lengthwise and place in a saucepan with the milk. Bring to simmer, then remove from heat. Cover and let stand to infuse.

VANILLA CUSTARD WITH CARAMEL SAUCE

❧ Place half the sugar in a small saucepan. Add the lemon juice and water and bring to boil. Cook until an amber-colored caramel forms. Remove from heat and pour the caramel into a 2-qt (2-l) metal charlotte mold, soufflé dish or cake tin; it may also be divided among individual soufflé dishes. Quickly turn the mold in your hands so the caramel coats the bottom and sides.

❧ Break the eggs into a large bowl and add the remaining sugar. Whisk until well blended, then whisk in the hot milk. Put the mixture into the mold through a fine sieve.

❧ Place the mold in a *bain-marie* (water bath) and bake for 1 hour (45 minutes for individual molds), or until the custard is set and a knife inserted in the center comes out clean.

❧ Remove the *crème caramel* from the water bath and let cool. Unmold onto a plate and serve at room temperature or cold. If it is to be served cold, keep refrigerated until serving time, then plunge the bottom of the mold into hot water for 30 seconds before unmolding.

Serves 6–8

Bretagne

TARTE AUX FRAISES
STRAWBERRY TART

10 oz (300 g) sweet pastry (recipe page 121)
⅔ cup (6½ oz/200 g) raspberry jam
2 tablespoons water
2 lb (1 kg) strawberries

❧ Preheat an oven to 425°F (215°C). Butter a 10-in (26-cm) tart plate (flan tin). Roll out the pastry into a 12-in (30-cm) circle and line the plate with it. Line with parchment paper and fill with dried beans or pie weights. Bake the pastry for 15 minutes, then remove the beans and paper and bake until the bottom is golden, about 20 minutes. Cool the tart shell on a wire rack. (The shell may be prepared several hours in advance.)

❧ An hour before serving time, combine the raspberry jam and water in a small saucepan and cook over low heat until the jam melts. Remove from heat and let cool. Wash, drain and hull the strawberries. Dry with paper towels and refrigerate.

❧ Fifteen minutes before serving, arrange the strawberries in the pastry shell, pointed ends up. Coat with the cooled jam and serve.

Serves 8

Alsace

TARTE AUX POMMES À L'ALSACIENNE
ALSATIAN APPLE TART

10 oz (300 g) sweet pastry (recipe page 121)
1 lb (500 g) Golden Delicious or pippin apples
4 egg yolks
⅓ cup (3 oz/90 g) sugar
1 envelope vanilla sugar or 3 drops vanilla extract (essence)
4 pinches cinnamon
¾ cup (6 fl oz/200 ml) heavy (double) cream

❧ Preheat an oven to 425°F (215°C). Butter a 10-in (26-cm) deep tart plate (flan tin). Roll out the pastry dough into a 12-in (30-cm) circle and line the plate with it.

❧ Peel, quarter and core the apples. Cut each quarter into 4 slices. Arrange evenly over the pastry in the form of a rose, starting from the outside and overlapping the slices slightly. Bake for 15 minutes.

❧ Meanwhile, combine the egg yolks, sugar, vanilla sugar and cinnamon and beat well. Beat in the cream. Coat the apples with this mixture and bake for another 35 minutes or until the apples are tender. Serve warm.

Serves 6

STRAWBERRY TART (TOP) AND ALSATIAN
APPLE TART (BOTTOM)

PUFF PASTRY WITH ALMOND FILLING

Orléanais

PITHIVIERS
PUFF PASTRY WITH ALMOND FILLING

1¼ lb (600 g) puff pastry (recipe page 122)

FOR THE FILLING:
1¼ cups (5 oz/150 g) ground blanched
 almonds
1¼ cups (5 oz/150 g) powdered (icing) sugar
⅔ cup (5 oz/150 g) soft butter
2 eggs
2 tablespoons dark rum

FOR THE GLAZE:
1 egg yolk

1 tablespoon milk
2 tablespoons powdered (icing) sugar

⚜ To prepare the filling: mix the ground almonds and sugar in a small bowl. Cream the butter in a large bowl. Blend in the almond mixture, eggs and rum.

⚜ Preheat an oven to 425°F (215°C). Cut the puff pastry into 2 equal parts and roll out into two 12-in (30-cm) circles, using a large plate or cake pan as a guide. Hold the knife upright so that the pastry is not crushed, which would prevent it from rising evenly during baking.

⚜ Lightly moisten a baking sheet and lay one of the pastry circles on it. Spread with almond mixture to within ⅜ in (1 cm) of the edge. Place the second pastry disc on top of this, smooth side up (i.e., the side that was in contact with the work surface). Press firmly all around the edge of the pastry so that the two circles will stick together. Make small cuts in the edge of the *pithiviers* ⅜ in (1 cm) apart.

⚜ To prepare the glaze: beat the egg yolk and milk together and brush the mixture over the surface of the pastry; do not let it run over the edge, as this would prevent the pastry from rising as it bakes. Using the point of a knife, make very shallow curved cuts on the surface of the pastry, from the outside edge into the center.

⚜ Bake for 30 minutes. Sprinkle with powdered sugar and bake for 5 more minutes or until the surface is shiny and slightly caramelized. Transfer the pastry to a serving plate and serve warm.

Serves 6

PARIS–BREST

PRALINE BUTTER CREAM CAKE

A Paris pastry cook was watching the Paris-to-Brest cycling race passing in front of his shop in 1891 when he had the idea of creating this cake, which is ring-shaped like a bicycle wheel.

13 oz (400 g) choux pastry (recipe page 120)
1 egg white
½ cup (2 oz/60 g) slivered (flaked) almonds

FOR THE FILLING:
1⅓ cups (11 oz/350 ml) milk
3 egg yolks
⅓ cup (3 oz/90 g) superfine (caster) sugar
½ vanilla bean (pod)
⅔ cup (3 oz/90 g) all-purpose (plain) flour
⅔ cup (3½ oz/100 g) powdered praline (see below)
⅓ cup (3 oz/90 g) soft butter
2 tablespoons powdered (icing) sugar

FOR THE PRALINE:
⅓ cup (2 oz/60 g) almonds, coarsely chopped
¼ cup (2 oz/60 g) sugar
3 drops lemon juice

❧ Preheat an oven to 425°F (215°C). Lightly oil a nonstick baking sheet. Place an 8-in (20-cm) plate in the center of it. Place the choux pastry dough into a pastry bag fitted with a plain ¾-in (1.5-cm) tip and pipe a circle of pastry around the edge of the plate. Remove the plate and pipe another circle of pastry inside the first one, then pipe a third circle overlapping the first two. Lightly beat the egg white with a fork until frothy and brush over the pastry. Scatter the slivered almonds over. Bake for 15 minutes, then lower the heat to 375°F (190°C) and bake for 15 minutes longer.

❧ Meanwhile, prepare the filling: bring the milk to boil in a small saucepan. Combine the egg yolks, sugar and vanilla bean in a large saucepan and whisk until the mixture turns pale in color. Add the flour and mix again. Whisk in the boiling milk. Place over moderate heat and cook the custard, beating constantly, until it thickens. Let it boil for 1 minute, then remove from heat and let cool, stirring occasionally. When cool, add the praline and then the butter, beating by hand for 2 minutes. Refrigerate.

❧ To make the praline: in a dry pan over medium heat, lightly brown the almonds for 5 minutes. In a separate pan melt the sugar with the lemon juice to make a light caramel. Add the almonds and mix for 2 minutes until the caramel darkens. Pour onto a marble slab and let cool completely. Break the caramel and pound or grind to a fine powder.

❧ Let pastry stand in the turned-off oven for 10 minutes with the oven door slightly ajar. Remove from the oven and let cool. Cut the pastry in two horizontally, a third of the way from the top; the bottom part, which is to be filled, must be higher.

❧ Place the cooled filling in a pastry bag fitted with a fluted ¾-in (2-cm) tip. Fill the bottom of the pastry with the custard, letting it overlap the edges slightly. Replace the top third of the pastry. Sprinkle with powdered sugar and keep in a cool place until serving time.

Serves 6   *Photograph pages 108–109*

CREAM HORNS (TOP) AND MADELEINES (BOTTOM)

Lorraine

MADELEINES DE COMMERCY
MADELEINES

Stanislas Leszczynski, Marie Leszcynska's cook, Talleyrand's cook Avice, and Mme. Perrotin de Barmond's cook, Madeleine Paulmier, have all been credited with the invention of the madeleine. This "little shell of cake, so generously sensual beneath the piety of its stern pleating," as Marcel Proust described it, remains, however, the uncontested specialty of the small town of Commercy.

PREVIOUS PAGES: SNOW EGGS (TOP LEFT, RECIPE PAGE 113), MERINGUES CHANTILLY (CENTER LEFT), PRALINE BUTTER CREAM CAKE (TOP RIGHT, RECIPE PAGE 107) AND ORANGE LIQUEUR CRÊPES (BOTTOM RIGHT, RECIPE PAGE 102)

3 eggs
¼ cup (2 oz/60 g) superfine (caster) sugar
½ teaspoon orangeflower water
¼ cup (2 oz/60 g) soft butter
⅓ cup (2 oz/60 g) all-purpose (plain) flour
1 tablespoon powdered (icing) sugar

❧ Preheat an oven to 375°F (190°C). Butter 20–24 madeleine tins, depending on size.
❧ Combine the eggs and sugar and beat until the mixture is pale in color. Stir in the orangeflower water and butter. Sift in the flour and fold in gently.
❧ Divide the batter among the molds, filling them ¾ full. Bake for 15 minutes or until the madeleines have risen and are lightly browned. Turn out, dust with powdered sugar and cool on a rack before serving.

Makes approximately 24 madeleines

Auvergne

CORNETS DE MURAT
CREAM HORNS

¼ cup (2 oz/60 g) butter
2 egg whites
6 tablespoons superfine (caster) sugar
½ cup (2 oz/60 g) all-purpose (plain) flour
1 tablespoon dark rum

FOR THE FILLING:
2½ cups (20 fl oz/600 ml) very cold heavy (double) cream
1 envelope vanilla sugar or ¼ teaspoon vanilla extract (essence)

❧ Preheat an oven to 375°F (190°C). Butter one large or two small baking sheets. Melt the butter in a small saucepan, then remove from heat and let cool.

❧ Beat the egg whites with a fork until frothy. Mix in the sugar. Sift in the flour and stir, then beat in the butter and rum. Drop the batter by tablespoonfuls onto the baking sheet(s); it will spread out slightly to form small circles.

❧ Bake for 8–10 minutes or until the pastry circles are just golden. Quickly form the hot wafers into cone shapes, inserting the point of the pastry into the neck of a bottle so it will hold its shape until it cools. Let cool completely.

❧ At serving time, whip the cream and vanilla sugar to soft peaks. Spoon into a pastry bag fitted with a small fluted tip and pipe into the cones.

❧ The cream horns may be prepared several hours in advance but should be served as soon as they are filled.

Serves 6

Ile - de - France

MERINGUES À LA CHANTILLY
MERINGUES CHANTILLY

During his exile in Alsace in 1720, Stanislas Leszczynski, the former king of Poland and a great gourmet, had the pastry cook Gasparini brought over from Switzerland. He created a cake that was called "meringue" after the Swiss village of Mehringen where he was born. As for the chantilly, it had been created earlier, in 1714, by a chef named Vatel who officiated in the château *at Chantilly.*

FOR THE MERINGUES:

4 egg whites
⅔ cup (5 oz/150 g) superfine (caster) sugar
¾ cup (3½ oz/100 g) powdered (icing) sugar

FOR THE CHANTILLY:

2 cups (16 fl oz/500 ml) very cold heavy (double) cream
2 tablespoons superfine (caster) sugar

❧ To prepare the meringues: preheat an oven to 225°F (110°C). Butter and flour a baking sheet. Beat the egg whites to soft peaks in a large mixing bowl. Gradually add ¼ cup (2 oz/60 g) superfine sugar and continue to beat until the mixture is smooth and shiny. Add the remaining superfine sugar and beat for another 2 minutes at low speed. Fold in the powdered sugar with a rubber spatula.

❧ Transfer the meringue to a pastry bag fitted with a ¾-in (2-cm) fluted tip and pipe onto the prepared baking sheet in small domes or swirls as desired.

❧ Bake the meringues for about 1 hour, without letting them brown. They should be ivory-colored; if they begin to brown, lower the heat. Remove the baked meringues with a metal spatula and let cool on a rack.

❧ To prepare the chantilly: shortly before serving, whip the cream with an electric mixer until firm. Add the sugar and beat until the cream forms soft peaks.

❧ Place the cream in a pastry bag fitted with a small smooth or fluted tip. Pipe it onto the flat side of one meringue and sandwich with a second meringue. Continue with the remaining meringues and cream. Serve at once.

Makes approximately 16

Île-de-France

OEUFS À LA NEIGE
SNOW EGGS

1 vanilla bean (pod)
1 qt (1 l) whole milk
8 eggs, separated
⅔ cup (5 oz/150 g) superfine (caster) sugar

FOR THE CARAMEL:

⅓ cup (3 oz/90 g) superfine (caster) sugar
3 tablespoons water

❧ Split the vanilla bean lengthwise and place in a saucepan with the milk. Bring to boil, then remove from heat, cover and let stand to infuse. Place the egg whites in a large bowl and the yolks in a large saucepan.

❧ Sprinkle ⅔ of the sugar over the yolks, beating with a whisk or hand beater until the mixture is very pale in color. Beat in the hot milk. Place over low heat and cook, stirring constantly, until the custard coats the spoon. Remove from heat. Strain the mixture into a bowl and let cool, stirring from time to time.

❧ Beat the egg whites until very stiff, then beat in the remaining sugar; continue beating until the mixture is the consistency of meringue. Bring several inches of water to boil in an 11-in (28-cm) sauté pan, then reduce the heat so that it barely simmers.

❧ Dip a large, long-handled spoon into cold water, then scoop spoonfuls of the egg white from the bowl and place one by one into the simmering water; plunge the spoon into cold water beforehand so that the egg white will slide off easily. Turn each spoonful after 30 seconds and cook for 30 seconds on the other side. When the whites are cooked, use a skimmer to remove them from the water. Set on a wire rack that is covered with a cloth, not touching one another.

❧ To serve, pour the custard into a bowl and pile the cooked egg whites on it in a dome shape. To prepare the caramel, cook the sugar and water in a saucepan over gentle heat to form an amber-colored syrup. Pour over the eggs in a thin stream and serve at once.

Serves 6   *Photograph pages 108–109*

Anjou

CREMETS
CREAM MOLDS WITH FRUIT

1½ cups (12 fl oz/400 ml) heavy (double) cream
2 egg whites
superfine (caster) sugar
chilled heavy (double) cream
red fruits, such as strawberries, raspberries and/or red currants

❧ Whip the cream until it forms soft peaks. Whisk the egg whites until stiff but not dry. Gently whisk together the two ingredients.

❧ Line 4 round or heart-shaped perforated molds with cheesecloth (muslin). Each should be large enough to hold a quarter of the mixture. Divide the mixture among them and fold the corners of the cheesecloth over the top. Set the molds on a plate and refrigerate for 3 hours.

❧ Fold back the corners of the cheesecloth. Unmold each *cremet* onto a dessert plate and remove the cloth. Serve with sugar to taste, cream, and fruits of your choice.

Serves 4

TARTE AU CITRON
LEMON TART

8 oz (250 g) sweet pastry (recipe page 121)

FOR THE FILLING:
3 lemons
4 eggs
½ cup (4 oz/125 g) butter
1 cup (7 oz/220 g) superfine (caster)
   sugar

❖ Preheat an oven to 425°F (215°C). Butter a 9-in (24-cm) tart plate (flan tin). Roll out the dough to an 11-in (28-cm) circle and line the tart plate with it. Line with parchment paper and fill with dried beans or pie weights. Bake for 15 minutes.

❖ Meanwhile, prepare the filling: wash and dry lemons. Grate the rinds into a bowl. Halve the lemons and squeeze out the juice; pour ¾ cup (6 fl oz/200 ml) of the juice into the bowl. Separate 3 of the eggs. Combine the yolks and whole egg and beat with a fork. Place the whites in a larger bowl.

❖ Melt the butter in a saucepan, add ¾ cup (6 oz/185 g) of the sugar and mix well. Add the egg yolk and lemon mixtures and cook over low heat, beating constantly, for 5 minutes or until the mixture thickens. Strain into a large bowl and let cool.

❖ Remove the beans and paper from the tart shell and bake until browned, about 10 more minutes. Pour in the lemon filling. Beat the egg whites until very stiff, then beat in the remaining sugar to form a meringue. Spread the meringue evenly over the surface of the tart, using either a large spoon or a piping bag with plain tip. Return the tart to the oven for 10–15 minutes or until the meringue is golden. Let cool completely before serving.

Serves 6   *Photograph page 6*

BABA
RUM BABA

Finding the kugelhopf *too dry for his taste, Stanislas Leszczynski had the idea of moistening it with Malaga wine. He christened the new dish "Ali Baba" in honor of his favorite book,* The Thousand and One Nights. *Subsequently it became known simply as a* baba, *and the Malaga wine was replaced by rum.*

3 teaspoons sugar
¼ cup (2 fl oz/60 ml) warm water
1 envelope (½ oz/15 g) dry yeast
3 tablespoons milk
¼ cup (2 oz/60 g) butter
¾ cup (4 oz/125 g) all-purpose (plain) flour
2 eggs
3 pinches salt

FOR THE SYRUP:
¾ cup (6½ oz/200 g) sugar
1½ cups (12 fl oz/400 ml) water
6 tablespoons (3 fl oz/90 ml) dark rum

❖ Place 1 teaspoon sugar in a 1-cup (8–fl oz/250-ml) measure. Add the warm water and stir until the sugar dissolves. Sprinkle the yeast over the surface and let stand in a warm place for about 10 minutes or until the mixture has risen almost to the top of the cup.

❖ Meanwhile, heat the milk to lukewarm in

RUM BABA, SERVED WITH WHIPPED CREAM

a small saucepan. Work the butter with a wooden spoon until creamy. Sift the flour into a mixing bowl and make a well in the center. Add the eggs, salt, the remaining sugar, the milk and the yeast mixture to the well and mix. Add the butter and mix again. Knead the dough until smooth and elastic, lifting it as high as possible and letting it fall to force in as much air as possible.

❖ Butter a 9-in (24-cm) *baba* mold and place the dough in it. Cover with a cloth and let rise until level with the edge of the mold, about 1 hour.

❖ Preheat an oven to 400°F (200°C). Bake the *baba* for 25 minutes.

❖ Meanwhile, prepare the syrup: combine the sugar and water in a saucepan and bring to boil. Remove from heat and stir in the rum.

❖ When the *baba* is baked, turn it out onto a serving plate. Prick it all over and spoon the syrup over, scooping up the syrup that runs down onto the plate and spooning it back over the cake until it is soaked all over. Refrigerate for at least 4 hours before serving.

Serves 6

PEAR CAKE

Anjou

POIRIER D'ANJOU

PEAR CAKE

1 cup (8 oz/250 g) sugar
2 cups (16 fl oz/500 ml) water
1 vanilla bean (pod), halved lengthwise
2 lb (1 kg) large perfumed pears
⅓ cup (3 oz/90 g) butter
¾ cup (6 fl oz/200 ml) milk

1¼ cups (6½ oz/200 g) all-purpose (plain)
   flour
2 teaspoons baking powder
2 eggs
2 tablespoons red currant jelly
3 tablespoons Cointreau

❧ Place ⅓ cup (3 oz/90 g) sugar in a large saucepan. Add the water and vanilla bean and bring to boil over low heat. Halve, peel and core the pears. Place the pear halves in the boiling syrup and cook for 30 minutes or until just tender. Drain, reserving the syrup.

✤ Preheat an oven to 425°F (215°C). Melt the butter in a small saucepan and let cool slightly. Butter a 9-in (24-cm) cake pan. Combine the flour and baking powder in a food processor. Add the eggs, the remaining sugar, the butter and milk and blend to form a smooth batter. Pour into the cake pan. Cut each pear half vertically into slices ⅜ in (1cm) thick and arrange on top of the batter in a rose pattern, starting from the center. Bake for 40 minutes or until a tester inserted in the center comes out clean.

✤ Meanwhile, boil the syrup in which the pears were cooked over high heat until very thick and syrupy. Add the red currant jelly and boil for 1 minute more. Add the Cointreau and remove from heat.

✤ Coat the cake with this syrup and bake for another 5 minutes. Unmold onto a serving plate. Serve warm or cold.

Serves 6

Provence

Tourte aux Blettes

Swiss Chard Pie

13 oz (400 g) sweet pastry (recipe page 121)
1½ lb (800 g) Swiss chard greens (silverbeet)
2 eggs
½ cup (3½ oz/100 g) firmly packed brown sugar
2 oz (60 g) Edam, Gouda or Emmenthaler cheese, freshly and finely grated
⅔ cup (3 oz/90 g) currants
½ cup (2½ oz/75 g) pine nuts
1 teaspoon grated lemon rind
freshly ground pepper
1 egg yolk
1 tablespoon milk

✤ Preheat an oven to 400°F (200°C). Butter an 8-in (22-cm) deep-sided ovenproof china pie plate. Divide the dough in two, one piece a little larger than the other. Roll out the larger piece into a 10-in (25-cm) circle and line the pie plate with it.

✤ Wash the chard and place in a very large pot with the water still clinging to the leaves. Cover and cook over high heat for 5 minutes. Drain in a colander and let cool. Squeeze the chard between your hands to get rid of as much moisture as possible, then chop it coarsely.

✤ Break the eggs into a mixing bowl and beat in the sugar with a fork. Add the cheese, chard, currants, pine nuts, lemon rind and pepper and mix well. Pour this filling into the pastry shell. Using a pastry brush, moisten the edge of the pastry with water, then lay the remaining pastry over the top of the filling and crimp the edges of the pastry to seal.

✤ Beat the egg yolk and milk and brush the entire surface of the pie with this mixture. Bake for 45 minutes or until the crust is golden. Let the pie cool for 10 minutes before turning it out onto a wire rack. Serve at room temperature.

Serves 6
Photograph page 6

BISCUIT DE SAVOIE
SAVOY SPONGE

1 cup (8 oz/250 g) superfine (caster) sugar
7 eggs, separated
2 teaspoons vanilla extract (essence) or the
  grated rind of 1 lemon
¾ cup (3½ oz/100 g) all-purpose (plain) flour
¾ cup (3½ oz/100 g) potato starch (potato
  flour)
1 tablespoon powdered (icing) sugar

❧ Preheat an oven to 280°F (140°C). Butter
and flour a 9-in (24-cm) round cake pan.
❧ Combine the sugar, egg yolks and vanilla
and beat with an electric mixer at high speed
until the mixture is pale in color and tripled
in volume. Sift the flour and potato starch and
fold in. Beat the egg whites to stiff peaks and
fold quickly into the batter.
❧ Spread the batter in the prepared pan and
bake for 50 minutes or until the cake is
golden brown and a tester inserted in the
center comes out clean.
❧ Turn off the oven and let the cake rest for
10 minutes in the oven with the door open,
then turn out of the pan onto a wire rack to
cool completely. Sprinkle with powdered
sugar before serving.
❧ The sponge may be eaten as is or filled
with chocolate cream, jam, pastry cream or
custard. It can also be used as a base for any
kind of charlotte.

Serves 6

SAVOY SPONGE (TOP) AND
GRENOBLE CARAMEL WALNUT CAKE (BOTTOM)

GRENOBLOIS
GRENOBLE CARAMEL WALNUT CAKE

1¼ cups (10 oz/300 g) butter
2 cups (8 oz/250 g) walnuts
6 eggs, separated
1 cup (7 oz/200 g) superfine (caster) sugar
3 tablespoons dark rum
1 teaspoon coffee extract (or 1 teaspoon
  instant coffee dissolved in 1 teaspoon water)
¾ cup (3 oz/90 g) dry breadcrumbs
⅓ cup (3 oz/90 g) sugar
6 tablespoons (3 oz/90 ml) water
½ teaspoon fresh lemon juice
walnuts

❧ Preheat an oven to 400°F (200°C). Butter a
9-in (24-cm) round cake pan. Melt the butter
over low heat in a small saucepan and let cool.
Finely chop the walnuts in a food processor.
❧ Combine egg yolks with ⅔ cup (5 oz/150 g)
superfine (caster) sugar and whisk until the
mixture doubles in volume and is pale in color,
about 10 minutes. Fold in butter, rum and
coffee extract, then breadcrumbs and walnuts.
❧ Beat the egg whites to soft peaks, then
gradually add the remaining superfine (caster)
sugar and beat until smooth and shiny. Gently
fold the egg whites into the walnut mixture.
Pour the batter into the prepared pan and
bake until browned, about 35 minutes.
❧ Combine ⅓ cup (3 oz/90 g) sugar, water
and lemon juice in a small saucepan and bring
to boil. Cook until a dark caramel forms.
❧ Turn the cake out onto a serving plate.
Pour the caramel over and decorate with
walnuts. Let cool completely before serving.

Serves 8

BASIC RECIPES

BOUILLON DE VOLAILLE
CHICKEN STOCK

This delicate, aromatic stock is used in the preparation of many dishes. It may be frozen in small containers for future use.

4 lb (2 kg) chicken carcasses and bones
1 small onion
1 clove
8 cups (2 qt/2 l) cold water
1 carrot, peeled
1 celery stalk
1 leaf of leek
1 sprig dried thyme
1 bay leaf
½ teaspoon sea salt
12 black peppercorns

❧ Wash carcasses and bones under running water. Stud the onion with the clove. Place the carcasses and bones in a large pot. Add the cold water and bring to boil over low heat, skimming off the first brown scum. Add the vegetables, thyme, bay leaf, salt and pepper and simmer gently, half covered, for 2 hours or until reduced to about 4¾ cups (1.2 l). Strain.

Makes approximately 4¾ cups (1.2 l) stock

PÂTE BRISÉE
SHORT (SHORTCRUST) PASTRY

1 cup (5 oz/150 g) all-purpose (plain) flour
⅓ cup (3 oz/100 g) soft butter
1½ tablespoons water
½ teaspoon salt

❧ If possible, prepare the pastry the day before, so that it loses all elasticity and is easy to roll out.
❧ Place the flour, butter, water and salt in the bowl of a food processor. Mix for 30 seconds, or until the pastry comes together into a ball. Wrap the ball of dough in plastic wrap, without further kneading, and chill thoroughly. Remove the pastry from the refrigerator an hour before it is to be used, and let rest at room temperature.
❧ Roll out pastry on a lightly floured surface according to instructions in recipe; transfer to pan. If possible, return pan to the refrigerator for an hour before baking; although this is not absolutely necessary, the pastry will cook better if prechilled.

Makes approximately 8 oz (250 g) pastry

PÂTE À CHOUX
CHOUX PASTRY

1 cup (5 oz/150 g) all-purpose (plain) flour
1 cup (8 fl oz/250 ml) water
2 teaspoons sugar
1 teaspoon salt
⅓ cup (3 oz/90 g) butter
5 eggs

❧ Sift the flour into a large bowl. Combine the water, sugar, salt and butter in a saucepan over low heat and bring just to boil. Remove from heat. Pour in all the flour, stirring quickly with a wooden spoon.
❧ Return the saucepan to the stove and stir over low heat for 1 minute longer to dry out the mixture. Remove from heat and beat in the eggs one at a time, completely incorporating each before the next is added. Once the last

egg has been mixed in, stop stirring; this helps produce smooth, uniform puffs. The finished pastry may be used immediately or wrapped in plastic and refrigerated for several days.

Makes approximately 1 lb 10 oz (800 g) pastry

PÂTE SUCRÉE

SWEET SHORT (SHORTCRUST) PASTRY

½ cup (4 oz/125 g) soft butter
⅓ cup (3 oz/90 g) superfine (caster) sugar
1 egg
1⅔ cups (8 oz/250 g) all-purpose (plain) flour
2 pinches salt

✤ Cream the butter and sugar until pale and fluffy. Add the egg and mix for 30 seconds. Add the flour and salt and mix until a smooth dough forms.

✤ Place the pastry on a work surface and knead, pushing it out with the palm of the hand, then reforming it into a ball, until the dough is smooth and elastic; this should take about 5 minutes. Wrap the ball of dough in plastic and refrigerate for at least 2 hours, preferably longer. Remove from the refrigerator 1 hour before using. Any leftover pastry can be stored in the refrigerator for 4 days or frozen.

✤ The egg will prevent this pastry from becoming soggy, even when cooked directly with the filling. It may also be baked blind, in large or small pans, by covering the pastry with waxed or parchment paper and filling it with rice, dried beans or pie weights.

Makes approximately 1 lb (500 g) pastry

PÂTE À PAIN

BREAD DOUGH

1 teaspoon superfine (caster) sugar
6 tablespoons (3 fl oz/100 ml) lukewarm water
1 envelope (½ oz/15 g) dry yeast
3¼ cups (1 lb/500 g) all-purpose (plain) flour
1½ teaspoons salt
⅔ cup (5 fl oz/150 ml) lukewarm milk

✤ Place the sugar in a teacup. Add the water and stir until the sugar is dissolved. Sprinkle the yeast over, stir in, and let rise in a warm place for about 10 minutes, or until the mixture reaches the edge of the cup.

✤ Sift the flour onto a work surface and sprinkle with salt. Mix the two together and make a well in the middle. Pour in the milk and the yeast mixture.

✤ Mix all ingredients together, using the fingertips in a quick movement from the center to the edges, then roll the dough into a ball. Knead it by stretching out the dough in front of you, then folding it in two, giving it a quarter turn in a counterclockwise direction and repeating the operation. Continue to knead the dough in this way for about 10 minutes, or until it is smooth, elastic and no longer sticky.

✤ Place the dough in a floured bowl and cover with a clean, damp towel. Let rise in a warm draft-free area until doubled in volume, about 1½ hours.

✤ Turn the risen dough onto a floured work surface and flatten with the palm of the hand, then knead as before for about 3 minutes. The dough is then ready for use.

Makes approximately 1½ lb (750 g) dough

PÂTE FEUILLETÉE

PUFF PASTRY

1 lb (500 g) soft butter
3¼ cups (1 lb/500 g) all-purpose (plain)
   flour
1 teaspoon salt
about 1 cup (8 fl oz/250 ml) water

❧ Remove the butter from the refrigerator 1 hour before using. In a large bowl, cream the butter until smooth and soft. Sift the flour onto a work surface. Make a well in the center and add the salt and ¾ of the water. Blend the flour and water together with the fingertips of one hand, while the other hand gradually pushes the flour from the edges toward the center. Working with the fingertips, gradually blend in just enough of the remaining water to make a dough of the same consistency as the creamed butter; this dough is called *détrempe*. Roll it into a ball and let rest for 15 minutes.

❧ Roll out the *détrempe* on a floured work surface to form a circle ¾ in (2 cm) thick and 6 in (15 cm) in diameter. With moistened fingers, spread the butter, in a layer again about ¾ in (2 cm) thick, in the center of the circle. Fold the edges of the dough over the butter, allowing an overlap of ¾ in (2 cm). You will now have a kind of envelope enclosing the butter; this is called the *pâton*. Dust both the *pâton* and the rolling pin with flour and roll out the *pâton* to a rectangle approximately 12 by 4 in (30 by 10 cm); apply only light pressure to the *pâton* so that it rolls out smoothly and the butter is not squeezed out.

❧ Now the operation known as *tourage* begins. Lift the lower edge of the pastry and fold it over to 4 in (10 cm) from the opposite edge. Press down this fold lightly with the rolling pin. Fold the remaining third of the pastry over the two layers and again lightly press down with the rolling pin: the pastry has just been given its first *tour,* or turn. The *tours* are done two at a time, but the *pâton* must always be turned a quarter of a circle, in a clockwise direction, so that the folds are no longer at the top and bottom, but on the left and right. Once more, roll out the *pâton* and fold it in thirds; it has now been given another turn. With the thumb and index finger, make two small indentations on the surface of the rectangle to indicate that the pastry has had two turns. Cover with a tea towel and refrigerate for 20 minutes.

❧ Give the pastry two more turns as before, making four indentations with the fingers to show that the pastry has had four turns. Classic puff pastry is given six turns, but it is preferable to give the last two just before the pastry is to be used. After four turns, the pastry should rest for at least another 20 minutes; it may be kept in the refrigerator for 48 hours before use.

❧ After the sixth turn, roll out the pastry and cut as required. When cutting the pastry, the knife should be kept vertical to avoid breaking the fine layers and allow maximum rise during baking. Puff pastry is always baked on a moistened, not buttered, baking sheet.

Makes approximately 2 lb 6 oz (1.2 kg) pastry

GLOSSARY

ANCHOVIES, SALTED OR IN OIL: Salted anchovies are fresh anchovies preserved in brine. They are sold by weight. Anchovies in oil are salted anchovies separated into fillets, rinsed, drained and marinated in oil. They are sold in tins or jars.

ARAIGNÉE: This long-legged crab—hence its name, spider crab or *maia squinado*—is caught in the Mediterranean and the Atlantic, especially in Aquitaine and the Basque region. Its firm, fine-textured and delicate flesh is much appreciated.

ARMAGNAC: A spirit, distilled from wine, which is produced in a defined area of Gascogne, essentially within the *département* of Gers. The region is divided into three areas of production: Bas-Armagnac, which produces a first-class brandy; Ténéraze, with its fragrant brandies; and Haut-Armagnac, where the brandies are less well defined. Armagnac is labeled *"monopole," "selection"* or *"trois étoiles"* (three stars) if it has been aged for at least a year; "VO" (very old), "VSOP" (very superior old pale) or *"réserve"* after at least four years of aging; and "extra," *"napoléon," "vieille réserve"* (old reserve) or *"hors d'âge"* when aged for more than five years. Armagnac is excellent for drinking at the end of a meal and is also used in many main dishes and desserts to add strength and aroma.

ARTICHOKE: The large Breton artichoke is always eaten cooked, while the small purple artichoke of Provence is superb whether cooked or not, like the little *poivrade* artichokes that are munched raw.

BAGUETTE: This is the most familiar form of French bread. It is a long, crusty stick weighing 8 oz (250 g), most commonly prepared with bleached white flour.

BASIL: This herb has symbolized Mediterranean cuisine since the invention of *pistou*. There are several varieties, with smaller or larger leaves and with a more or less pronounced flavor. A decorative purple basil is also available.

BEANS: Broad bean: Known for thousands of years, broad beans are most particularly appreciated in all the southern parts of France. Fresh in summer and autumn, they are sold in shells enclosing between five and ten beans of a green color, covered with a skin which must be removed before eating them, raw or cooked. Dried broad beans are also available; they must be soaked before cooking, like other dried beans.

Haricots verts: French green beans are cultivated mostly in the Val de Loire and in Provence, and are eaten from late spring until late fall. Several sizes are available, from thick to extra thin; the thinnest beans are considered the tastiest.

Flageolets: These beans are found ready to be shelled in all markets during late summer and in the fall. Out of season, they can be purchased dried and should then be soaked for about 12 hours before cooking. These pretty beans, of a delicate green color, can be replaced by any other shelled white beans—navy beans, for example.

BOUQUET GARNI: A combination of herbs and flavorings tied together and used to flavor stocks and simmered dishes. The basic composition includes thyme, bay leaf and parsley, but according to the region and the type of dish, it might also include celery stalks, branches of fennel, leek leaves or orange rind.

BROUSSE DE BREBIS: As the name implies, this is a ewe's milk cheese. It comes fresh in a hemispherical shape, drained in wicker baskets or, today, in plastic cartons. The cheese is white, soft, very mild and flavorful. It is just as delicious in savory preparations (stuffings, tarts) as in desserts (cakes, mousses, charlottes).

BUTTER: A very important ingredient in French cuisine, particularly delicious when farm-made from unpasteurized milk. Most often it is sold in pasteurized form. It is important to differentiate unsalted butter from *demi-sel* or lightly salted butter, a Breton specialty. The best unsalted butters come from Normandie, Charentes and Deux-Sèvres.

CALVADOS: A spirit distilled in Normandie from cider. It is very good used in cooking, and excellent for adding an apple flavor to cakes and pastries. In Bretagne and Normandie a *"café-calva"* is served: the *calvados* comes with the coffee and is either drunk after it or poured into the hot coffee before drinking.

CANTAL: A cheese with 45 percent fat, produced in Auvergne from cow's milk. It is semisoft and comes in the form of a cylinder about 16 in (40 cm) in diameter and 16 in (40 cm) high, weighing about 40 kg. The greyish crust hides a pale-colored cheese, firm and somewhat crumbly, its flavor slightly biting.

CAYENNE PEPPER: A fine red powder often known simply as "cayenne," made from the dried and powdered fruits of the cayenne pepper. These slender, long, pointed and very hot fruits are known as "bird peppers" in the Antilles.

CHEESES: The varieties of French cheese are by now too numerous to mention. Some of them are used mainly as the final addition to a dish; Gruyère or Parmesan, for example, is simply grated over pasta or rice or used in various stuffings. Others, however, are an integral part of a recipe—for example, in Savoie *comté* cheese is used in the celebrated local soufflé and in chicken dishes (see recipes). We should also note the many regional recipes using Beaufort, goat cheese, *tomme* (made with cow's, goat's or ewe's milk depending on the region) or Roquefort (a ewe's milk cheese with veins of blue mold that develop during the aging process).

COGNAC: A spirit, distilled from wine, which is made in the area around Cognac, a town in Charentes. Cognac is labeled *"trois étoiles"* (three stars) if it has aged for at least two years; "VO" (very old), "VSOP" (very superior old pale) or *"réserve"* after at least five years of aging; and "extra," *"napoléon"* or *"vieille réserve"* (old reserve) when aged for more than seven years. Cognac is an excellent drink for the end of a meal; it is also used to add aroma to numerous main dishes and desserts. *"Fine Champagne"* or liqueur cognac is a blending of the first two cognac vintages (*Grande Champagne* and *Petite Champagne*), containing at least 50 percent *Grande Champagne*.

CRAYFISH: There are numerous varieties of this little freshwater crustacean, which looks like a miniature lobster. The most famous, and the tastiest (with flavor like a lobster), is the crayfish *à pattes rouges,* with red claws. Unfortunately it is becoming more and more rare in our rivers and is most often imported or farmed.

CRÈME FRAÎCHE: A mature cream with a nutty, slightly sour tang. It can be made by mixing two tablespoons of cultured buttermilk with two cups heavy cream; cover and let stand at room temperature until thick or leave overnight. Stir cream, then cover and refrigerate to thicken it further.

CRÉPINE: Caul fat, a very thin membrane with veins of white fat, which covers the internal organs of the pig. Used to wrap terrines and pâtés, it must always be soaked in warm water before use, to soften. Caul fat can be replaced by thin slices of fatty bacon.

CROUTONS: Small slices of bread fried in butter or oil, or simply toasted.

EMMENTHALER: A firm cheese, with 45 percent fat, prepared from cow's milk in Franche-Comté or Savoie. It comes as enormous wheels 32 in (80 cm) in diameter and 10 in (25 cm) high, weighing as much as 180 lb (90 kg). The crust is smooth and yellow, the cheese mild and fruity, with large holes.

FAISSELLE: A fresh cow's milk cheese, sold in a *faisselle* (hence its name), a sort of colander in which the cheese drains.

GARLIC: It is important to differentiate the new season type from garlic that has been stored. The former appears in the markets around the end of spring and is available until the end of summer; it has a white or purplish bulb and a long stalk. The peeled garlic clove is white, mild and fruity, easy to digest (because the germ has not developed) and aromatic. As it dries, its flavor becomes stronger and more noticeable. Garlic braids can be kept for a whole year in a cool, dry place. After fall, the soft green germ, or shoot, starts to develop in the heart of the cloves. It is indigestible and should be removed, either after the clove of garlic is cut in half or just before it is eaten cooked whole.

GOOSE FAT: This is the fat from inside the goose, melted and then strained. Sold in jars and tins, it is very popular in the cuisine of the southwestern regions. Once used, it may be strained and stored in the refrigerator in a tightly sealed container for about one month. Take care; goose fat quickly becomes rancid.

HERBES DE PROVENCE: A blend of dried herbs including thyme, rosemary, bay leaf, savory and lavender.

LANGOUSTINES: These little marine crustaceans—called *scampi* by the Italians and *gambas* by the Spaniards—are fished almost all year round along the Atlantic coast. The tail, from 10 to 15 in (15 to 30 cm) in length, has delicate flesh; the long pincers are almost without flesh. The langoustine's hue of pink, brick or salmon, marked with the finest of lines—showing its years—changes little in cooking.

MALAGA RAISINS: Large black grapes dried as a bunch. They are very moist, sweet and flavorsome.

MARC: After the grapes have been pressed for making wine, a solid mass of skins, seeds and stems remains; this is distilled into alcohol known as *marc*. Different wine-growing areas produce *marcs* of different flavors—for example, *marc de Bourgogne* and *marc de Champagne*.

MUSHROOMS, CULTIVATED: White or pink *champignons de Paris* are available all year round. They must always be selected very fresh, with the caps firmly attached around the stalks. The white ones are a uniform ivory color, the pink ones a pinkish-brown. Both tiny and very large mushrooms are excellent; the small ones are used in sautés and gently simmered dishes, while the large ones are often stuffed.

MUSHROOMS, WILD: Gathered in the fields and in woods, these mushrooms appear in French markets in spring and fall. Among the best known and most widely used are *cèpes* (boletus mushrooms or *porcini,* of which many varieties exist), the apricot-colored *girolles* (perhaps better known as *chanterelles*), morels, blewits, *pleurotes* (which these days are cultivated), *craterelles* (sometimes called in France "trumpets of death"), and of course truffles. They are often expensive and sometimes scarce and are most often served as a vegetable, sautéed briefly with garlic or shallots and sometimes with cream added. But they also add a wonderful flavor to all sorts of stews and simmered dishes. Abroad, and in France too, when out of season, they are often replaced by dried mushrooms.

OLIVE OIL: Extra virgin or first cold-pressed olive oil is derived from the first crushing of the olives, by mechanical means and not steam. This oil is natural, pure, fruity and unrefined, and it is the ideal oil for salads as well as for cooking.

OLIVES: Green or black, olives are always treated in brine before being sold. They are sold in brine, or marinated in oil with flavorings, loose or in jars. Niçoise olives are very small olives, macerated in oil and flavorings and prepared in the Nice region.

PÂTE À PAIN OR PÂTE LEVÉE: Bread dough. This may be made at home, and it freezes very easily. In France it can be bought ready-prepared from the bakery, for making bread, all kinds of savory or sweet tarts, and cakes such as brioches, babas, *kugelhopf,* etc.

PÂTE BRISÉE: Short pastry made from flour, butter, salt and water or milk. This is the simplest of French pastries, elastic and firm rather than delicate. Being fairly impermeable, it can be used for sweet or savory tart bases without precooking. It may be enriched with eggs, which make it still firmer.

PÂTE SABLÉE: Flour, butter, eggs, sugar, salt and water. This is a delicate, very crumbly pastry, which must be worked as little as possible. It is very rich and is excellent for sweet tarts and cookies. For an even richer flavor, ground almonds may be added.

PORC DEMI-SEL OR PORC SALÉ: Nearly all cuts of pork, such as shoulder, sparerib, rump, belly, flank, tail, feet, ears, etc., are salted. In the south, salted pork belly is referred to as *petit salé*. The salting is done with a pickling brine of salt, sugar, water and saltpeter, either by immersion or by injection with multiple needles. Salting times vary from one to six days; the longer the time, the saltier the meat will taste. Meat that has been salted for one day requires simply a rinse under running water; if it has been salted for several days, however, it should be soaked for 12 hours in several changes of water. If you do not have time to do this, you can blanch it for about 15 minutes in boiling salted water, then rinse it before cooking.

Meat can be salted at home, by rubbing it with coarse sea salt (flavored with thyme, rosemary, bay leaf or crushed peppercorns if you wish) and then keeping it buried in additional coarse sea salt in the refrigerator, where it will keep for six days. You must take care that it is always covered with salt; if the salt dissolves, add more. Rinse off the salt under running water and leave the meat to soak, or else blanch it before using.

PORK RIND: This must be trimmed of all fat and blanched before using, particularly in slow-simmered dishes. It gives a marvelous syrupy, slightly gelatinous consistency to the sauce base.

PRALINE: Almonds cooked in caramel. Once cooked, the mixture is spread on a marble slab and cooled, then crushed to powder.

QUATRE-ÉPICES: A blend of spices used in France for many years to flavor meat terrines, pâtés and all kinds of charcuterie products. It is made of equal quantities of powdered white pepper, nutmeg, cloves and ginger. According to the end use, chili, cinnamon or mace may also be added.

SAUSAGES: There are two different types of sausage. Dry ones are eaten as is, thinly sliced, with drinks before dinner, as a first course in sandwiches, with baguette or coarse country bread accompanied by butter and gerkins, and so on. Cooking sausages are made from ground meat and fat, either alone or with truffles or pistachios added; they may be smoked or unsmoked. They must always be pricked several times with a fork before being slowly poached in barely simmering water for about 20 minutes.

SHALLOTS: There are two varieties: pink shallots, simply called shallots, and the grey type. The former are more common and more frequently used; they are a pinkish-brown color and much less aromatic and milder in flavor than the grey variety. The latter are greyish-brown in color and are covered by several thick layers of skin.

STOCK: Used to poach fish fillets, prepare a *blanquette de veau* or poach pieces of beef suspended by a string, but just as important for cooking rice or making a soup. Stocks prepared from bouillon cubes or flavorings extracts are not perfect substitutes. If you have a little time to spare, make your own stocks. They can be frozen in 6-tablespoon (100-ml) portions in plastic bags.

TOMATO PURÉE: Tomatoes, cooked and reduced to a lightly concentrated purée. It is sold in cardboard packs. A flavorful natural product, it has many very practical uses.

TRUFFLE: There are two kinds of truffle, white and black. The white or Piedmontese truffle is rare in France; it grows under oaks and linden trees in winter, at a depth of 2–20 in (5–50 cm) beneath the ground and looks rather like a large potato ranging from grey to ocher in color. It is superb and very delicate. The black truffle, called the "black diamond" of cooking, is better known. This black tuber, which can measure up to 6 in (15 cm) in diameter, is covered with little pyramidal warts; it grows spontaneously and ripens throughout the winter and up to early spring underneath oak, ash and hazel trees. Today black truffles are cultivated in the Vaucluse and Périgord areas in plantations of truffle-producing oak trees. Fragrant and delicious, they form the basis of many special-occasion dishes. Out of season and abroad they are to be found bottled or canned.

VANILLA SUGAR: Superfine (caster) sugar flavored with natural vanilla (in which case it is called vanilla sugar) or artificial vanilla (in which case it is called vanillin sugar, vanillin being a synthetic vanilla flavoring). It can be bought in 15-lb (7.5-kg) envelopes in packs of five or ten. If you are unable to find it, you can make it yourself: to 1/2 cup (4 oz/125 g) sugar, add 1 tablespoon powdered vanilla or a vanilla bean split in two. Keep this in an airtight jar for several months; more vanilla may be added as desired.

VENTRÈCHE: Pork belly, salted, seasoned and formed into a roll. It should be cut into thin slices, like *poitrine fumée.* Most commonly used in the southwest.

VERMOUTH: a fortified wine, 18 percent alcohol, flavored with aromatic herbs. It may be red or white, dry or sweet. The dry white vermouth is the one most commonly used in cooking.

VINAIGRETTE: this sauce is a mixture of oil and vinegar or lemon juice, with the possible addition of salt and pepper. It is traditionally used to dress green salads but also for all kinds of *crudités,* vegetables, fish and cold meats. Various other ingredients may be added, such as chopped shallots, onions or fresh herbs, crushed garlic, crumbled anchovy fillets, chopped hard-cooked egg, *tapenade,* or various kinds of mustard. Different types of oil and vinegar may be used—walnut, hazelnut, olive or peanut (groundnut) oil, wine vinegar, cider vinegar or flavored vinegar.

INDEX